S\

MW00334613

WHAT YOUR DAD NEVER TAUGHT YOU ABOUT BUDGETING

PETER DUNN
(Pete the Planner)

WHAT YOUR DAD NEVER TAUGHT YOU ABOUT BUDGETING

PETER DUNN
(Pete the Planner)

© 2012
All rights reserved.
ISBN :978-0-9834588-1-4

First edition published   2006
Second Edition
Green Olive Books edition 2012

The author gratefully acknowledges permission
from Channel V Books to publish material previously
published in *60 Days to Change: A Daily How-
To Guide with Actionable Tips for Improving Your
Financial Life.*

Library of Congress Control Number: 2012942600

Interior and Cover Design: Lindsay Hadley

WHAT YOUR DAD NEVER TAUGHT YOU ABOUT BUDGETING

THIS BOOK IS FOR SARAH, MIKE D., AND ANYONE WHO WANTS TO CREATE A BETTER FINANCIAL LIFE.

Sarah, thank you for your love, and thank you for making me smile every day. Mike D., thanks for being such great role model and teacher. If everyone had a dad like you, this world would be a better place.

Since I am a father now, it's important my children, Ollie and Teddy, know this book is for them, too. Sometimes as parents we get so caught up trying to provide for our children that we forget to teach them the skills they will need for the future. I know one thing for sure, Ollie and Teddy will never be able to say that I didn't teach them about budgeting.

This book is also for Otis.

AUTHOR'S NOTE ABOUT THIS SECOND EDITION

WHAT YOUR DAD NEVER TAUGHT YOU ABOUT BUDGETING

launched my career. I am forever indebted to the words in this book. The original words in the original book were good, but not great. I have decided to release a second edition in order to make that leap to great. I was twenty-seven years old when I wrote the first edition. I wasn't yet a father, I didn't have a weekly radio show, and I hadn't appeared on a single television program.

The truth is that I started writing the original version of this book on a flight to Houston. I didn't want to talk to the guy seated next to me. Yes, I realize how rude that is. I whipped out my laptop, started punching at the keys, and told the guy that I was on a tight deadline from my publisher. Of course I wasn't on a deadline, I didn't have a publisher, and until those words fell out of my mouth, I wasn't a writer. Would I do the same thing five years later? Absolutely. I may be older, but I'm still me.

Since the original release of *What Your Dad Never Taught You About Budgeting*, I have discovered and researched many great new ways to teach you how to budget. This edition of *What Your Dad Never Taught You About Budgeting* has nothing to do with me, or my airplane fibs. This book is about you.

PREFACE

Let me begin by saying that the first five years of my career were spent telling clients they didn't need a household budget. Many times, as a person in the financial industry, I felt compelled to tell people what they wanted to hear. People generally don't want to take the time to complete a budget, so I wasn't going to upset them by urging them to do one.

The longer I've been in the industry, however, the more I've realized that a household budget is the best tool to build wealth. Too many people are concerned about investing too soon. Yet, the source of the dollars to invest comes from the disciplined practice of budgeting. As you will see, budgeting is all about forming habits and creating an awareness about your spending.

Many financial advisors don't care if you don't form a budget because they don't make any money when you make a budget. They sell products and services that assume you maximize your cash flow. They work around your lack of a budget. However, by doing this, advisors are only treating the symptoms and not the problem.

I did not have a household budget in place for the first five years of my career. Today, that is no longer the case. Anyone who recommends one thing and does another is not a person to be trusted.

THE WHY

I can look through my client list and tell you who has the greatest risk of marital discord. That would be a terrible thing for me to do, but how people interact with money can reveal the level of trust they hold with each other. I've guessed correctly too many times when it comes to marital problems relating to money.

Nothing is better in life than being on the same page as your significant other, living in harmony, working together to enrich each other's lives. This book was written not only to help you improve your financial situation, but also to help you improve your relationship with your significant other.

By the end of this book, you will know how to hold a monthly accountability meeting with your significant other. In addition, you will be able to employ the powers of P.E.T.E. (Patience. Equality. Teamwork. Effort.)

As you read, take time to consider your own financial situation and how it compares to what I believe is the ideal way to handle your monthly budget.

Sometimes we ignore problems and hope, even expect, that they'll go away. But untreated financial problems will not go away on their own. I assure you that you cannot ignore bad money habits, and I assure you that you cannot ignore your spouse's bad money habits.

MY MOTIVATION

In *Smart Talk*, Lou Tice claims, "What if your purpose for working was to give so much of what you have to cause the life of other people to improve greatly? Suppose that was 75 percent of your intent, and 15 percent was to make a good living, and 10 percent was to feel good yourself.

I can guarantee you this: if you focus with 75 percent of your intent on doing good for others, you will make more money and you will feel better about yourself. If you focus on making money and feeling good first, you won't do much good for other people."

These two powerful paragraphs were my motivation for writing this book. They were also my motivation for changing my business to one with a budget-planning platform. I no longer ignore people's lack of a budget.

I have found that people tend to ignore budgeting because they would rather focus on exciting things like investments and retirement accounts. But you can't let your 401(k) or the stock market distract you. You are capable of accomplishing all of your financial goals as long as you understand the basics of budgeting.

Enjoy the read. I enjoyed writing it.

–Pete the Planner

CHAPTER ONE

WHY BUDGETING MATTERS

"YEAH, WE
PLAYERS MAKE
A LOT OF
MONEY,
BUT WE SPEND
A LOT OF
MONEY, TOO."

-PATRICK EWING,
DURING THE 1998-1999
NBA WORK STOPPAGE

For a very long time, I hated budgeting. Check that: I hated what I thought budgeting was. I felt that my intelligence, proficiency in mathematics, and my dislike of structure were good enough reasons to resist budgeting. Truth be told, I hadn't even considered the concept of budgeting until I moved into my first home upon graduating from college.

My first budget was scrawled on a sheet of copy paper. It was raw. It was simple. And it was heartfelt. I had no idea what the hell I was doing. It was embarrassing: my family ran a successful business, I was a business administration major in college, I got my stockbroker license before graduating from college, and I was employed as a personal financial representative. Yet my dad had never talked to me about budgeting, my college didn't offer any household finance courses, my line of work at the time (stock brokerage) dealt with assets and rarely addressed income, and, as I learned, the financial industry doesn't care about budgeting. I was in the exact place where you may find yourself right now.

It seems like you should naturally know how to budget. You calculate your income, determine your spending on various expense categories, and then try to spend less than your income provides. But it's just not that simple. Budgeting isn't organic. Budgeting doesn't spontaneously occur. It's a challenging activity that doesn't happen until you decide that it needs to be an important part of your financial life.

And you will eventually get to this point. You will eventually decide that your financial life will be enhanced by simply having a budget. You can put this decision off as for long as you like, but you will, in the end, budget. A day doesn't go by that a new retiree is forced to budget for the first time. Fixed income and fixed expenses always force this decision.

I have helped new retirees negotiate this forced change for over a decade. Teaching a sixty-five-year-old how to budget can be very challenging. When you operate your entire adult life without a budget for nearly forty years, being forced to budget becomes a matter of financial survival.

Many young people, on the other hand, don't budget, as a result of over-confidence in their ability to earn income. We have become accustomed to constantly increasing incomes. We assume that our incomes will increase with age. This isn't true. U.S. Census Bureau statistics show that U.S. Median Household Income fell 2.9% in 2009. Of even greater concern is that average annual expenditures per consumer unit fell 2.8% in 2009 following an increase of 1.7% in 2008. This means that income fell more than consumer spending fell. America was still overspending during the most financially devastating time in recent history.

Your income is not guaranteed to go up. Your subliminal excuse for not budgeting is bogus. You must budget.

But this is where things get tricky. The word "budget" is used to describe several different types of activities and processes. Let's examine these.

1. BUDGET.-*n.* This word isn't as straightforward as you think. "Budget" can be used to describe anticipated spending, or it can be used to describe a comparison of your income and expenses. The difference often stops people before they get started. My first "budget" was a single snapshot of my expected expenses. But it stopped there. Stopping at the one-time snapshot is a very common yet troublesome mistake.

2. BUDGETING. -*v.* The actual possession or completion of a budget is not sufficient. In order to actually accomplish something, you must actively budget. As you will learn in *What Your Dad Never Taught You About Budgeting*, consistent attention to budgeting will lead to lifelong financial success. This isn't as tedious as it may seem. If you are willing dedicate twenty minutes per month to your finances, then you have a chance of living relatively stress-free.

IS IT TIME TO RELENT?

There are constant signs in your financial life that indicate you should be budgeting. These signs often appear in the form of financial adversity. If any of these things have happened to you, then it's time to get serious and start budgeting.

- Overdraft charges at your bank
- Credit card debt
- Financial stress
- Relationship problems regarding money
- Daily visits to your online banking account
- Personal debts to a family member or friend

You can either ignore these signs–which will eventually bring you back to the original predicament–or you can take stock now, and ask yourself a very important question:

"How did I get to this point?"

It's the million-dollar question you should ask yourself *right now*. In fact, you should ask yourself this question every time you're feeling desperate. You should ask yourself this question every time financially disastrous things happen to you.

The answer to this question isn't something most people want to hear. Because the answer is: You caused it. It's all your fault.

Yes, I realize this isn't exactly encouraging. But once you understand that your financial struggles *are* your fault, then you will quickly realize that your financial success is also controlled by your actions. If you can screw it up, you can fix it.

You control your financial destiny. Your life is not like Monopoly. In Monopoly, when you land on Chance or Community Chest you draw a card that reveals your immediate fate. That fate can be positive or negative, and you deal with it accordingly.

But somehow when these random events occur in real life, people tend to flip out. We know emergencies are going to occur, yet we're rarely prepared for them financially. Worse, people often look for someone else to blame when financial turmoil arises.

About once a year, I meet someone who is shocked to have to come up with some cash to replace the brakes on their car. This person is incredibly surprised, as though they'd awoken that morning with their head sewn to the pillow! As far as I know, no set of brakes lasts forever. Our lack of preparation for this moment is our fault. And if this sort of "emergency" tends to occur over and over again, it's time to change. *Financial mistakes don't appear in the emergency –they appear in the aftermath.* If you don't change your behavior, then you consistently will get the same undesired result.

Does this sound like something you face? Then you need to change. If you are reactive, as opposed to proactive, then you've got to change.

So gather up your financial disappointments. Gather up your financial failures. Gather up your financial excuses. It's time to get good results on a consistent, lifelong basis.

MAKE CHANGE HAPPEN

If you're tired of getting the same paltry results from the way you handle your finances, then change. Today. There's no reason to think that if you continue doing something that doesn't work, it eventually will lead to success. You are simply banging your head against a brick wall. Don't coast through your financial life. As Zig Ziglar, world renowned business guru, says, "The only way to coast is downhill." And downhill is not the direction you want to go.

FIVE
GREAT
REASONS
TO CHANGE

You have countless reasons
to take control of your financial
life, but I've summarized five
key reasons for you.

1. BLISSFUL AWARENESS.

There's no better feeling than to be in the know. Being on top of your budget opens the door to productive awareness. Very few people have full knowledge of their personal financial situation. But those who do are typically very successful.

Join them. You will know what you can afford, whether you should buy something, and how that purchase will affect your monthly budget.

2. SELF-CONTROL.

Once you take control of one area of your life, other critical areas will start to shape up. Self-control will bring progress. The possibilities are endless: a great financial life, great fitness, great relationships, great spiritual life, a great attitude. The concept of proper budgeting is not like dieting. While dieting often leads to craving certain foods, budgeting rarely leads to craving irrational spending. This is a lifestyle change.

3. RELATIONSHIP MIRACLES.

No matter how great your relationship is with your significant other, it can get better. Changing your level of commitment to your finances is an act of love. If you want to create a positive event, change the way you manage your money. This new way will open up the lines of communication forever. Get rid of all the nasty things that hurt communication and marital bliss–things like assumptions, embarrassment, and resentment.

4. PERSONAL RESPONSIBILITY.

Americans have gotten (earned) a soiled reputation over the past two decades. We spend more than we make and we tend to value accumulation over preservation. Will you complain about the way things are, or will you hold yourself accountable for everything you can control? The way to prevent your children from continuing on this irresponsible financial path is to take responsibility for your financial actions now.

I made a promise to myself years and years ago to never blame anyone for anything that happened to me. Was I being a martyr? Nope. I was giving myself power. The second you blame someone or something, you relinquish power to that entity. Why would you do that? By taking 100% responsibility for what happens to me, I have made better decisions and calculated risks more carefully. Have I run into some roadblocks? Absolutely. But I never waste any time trying to blame anyone because I already know that I am to blame. I simply start working on a solution. If you find yourself short on answers to your life's financial problems, then I challenge you to "own the problem." Take the power back from those people or places you blame. You will need this power and energy to fix your problems.

Let's briefly discuss the concept of blaming yourself. Here's what it's not: sitting in a dark room, drinking, and listening to Coldplay. Here's what blaming yourself is: gathering your wits, moving on, and forming a plan. A few years ago, my buddy Jason got laid-off from a manufacturing gig, along with several of his coworkers. While his former coworkers sat around and blamed the economy, the industry, and the company, Jason blamed himself. "I chose the wrong profession," he once told me. So he did his research, went back to school, and is now working a very stable and lucrative job as a registered nurse. On the flip side, I had a client blame his employer for his layoff for 2 years. He did nothing in the meantime...except ruin his marriage. "If XYZ corporation ruined my life, then XYZ needs to fix it" was his mantra. If you were to ask him what he does for a living, he would tell you he's a laid-off XYZ worker. Seriously. His wife got sick of his excuses, and she hit the road. She blamed herself.

5. A MACGYVER-FREE LIFESTYLE.

You may be hanging on by a thread. You may have been able to avoid bankruptcy up to this point. You may have a makeshift financial plan–but you're not MacGyver. You can't make a yo-yo into a bomb. You can't make a cell phone out of duct tape. And you can't make a successful financial plan with poor financial habits. Bad habits will catch up with you. And when they do, you won't be able to build a helicopter out of newspaper and a grilled-cheese sandwich and fly away from it all.

Now, get ready–because we are about to tackle these points, and many more like them. You are about to learn *What Your Dad Never Taught You About Budgeting.*

CHAPTER TWO
THE SKILLS TO PAY THE BILLS

SKILL- *N.* PROFICIENCY, FACILITY, OR DEXTERITY THAT IS ACQUIRED OR DEVELOPED THROUGH TRAINING OR EXPERIENCE.

I can't swim very well. I've never been able to swim very well. My body is not built for a Speedo–or for speed, for that matter.

I was on a swim team as a kid, and all the other kids would bet on whether I could finish my race before the next event started. Jesus may have walked on water, but I couldn't walk *in* water even if I was touching the bottom of the pool.

After swim practice, we would play "sharks and minnows." If you've never played it, it goes like this: one group of kids (the sharks) chases the other group of kids (the minnows).

As for me? I was the chum. My swim team even changed the name of the game to "sharks, minnows, and Pete the Chum." It was embarrassing–but my parents made me keep going until they were confident I knew how to swim. And it's true: the more I did swim, the better I got. But eventually I realized I just did not enjoy the practice of simulated drowning. So I learned barely enough skills to survive any water disaster short of the Titanic. Today, I'm content knowing that if I ever need those skills, I can confidently brush them off and embarrass myself to safety. Developing money skills can feel the same way, but these abilities are imperative to your financial survival. If you only develop your skills to the point of not drowning, you will end up treading water for years to come. And that will exhaust you and ultimately get you nowhere.

Everyone needs to develop money skills. The guy who makes millions of dollars a year is subject to the same fundamental responsibilities of efficient financial decision-making as the person who makes $30,000 per year. Copious assets and/or copious income are not an excuse for a lack of financial proficiency. Having advised several professional athletes, I've seen how a high income without financial discipline is actually a disadvantage.

We all have the power of choice. Whether you're choosing to create a budget or deciding what to have for dinner, you are responsible, ultimately, for the consequences. Lack of a budget at any income level can lead to financial ruin. Just as the wrong dinner choice can lead to a long night of indigestion.

INHERITING POOR FINANCIAL SKILLS

Our parents and grandparents didn't face all the problems we do today as we try to establish a financial foundation. The funny thing is that we brought these problems on ourselves by trying to simplify our lives. Our predecessors didn't have debit cards, lengthy credit terms, and interest-only loans. Rather, most of our grandparents (when they were our age) cashed their paychecks and put the household cash into different envelopes representing different budget categories. They'd pay bills out of those envelopes and always have enough money to cover the expense. It was hard for them to go backwards financially because they relied on cash. They couldn't, for example, buy fifty dollars of groceries with thirty dollars in cash.

What do we do now? We log onto our online banking accounts to see if we have enough money to cover the purchase we made earlier in the day. We spend first and worry about the consequences second. With this mentality, it doesn't matter if you are in the 1950s or 2050s, you're going to go broke.

Yes, managing your financial life is harder nowadays. Yes, peer pressure is worse than ever. And yes, some people make a lot more money than you. But if you are truly focused on bettering your life, you will ignore what's irrelevant. More money doesn't solve maladies caused by meager money management; more money only magnifies these money maladies. Mm-hmm!

Despite these money differences among generations, most of the skills you need to function financially were instilled in you by your parents. And sadly enough, this is the root of several problems. If your parents didn't know what they were doing, then your chances of innately knowing what you are doing are slim. And the problem gets worse when you factor in your parents' level of financial confidence. Your parents' financial aptitude can be classified into a few categories:

1. They knew what they were doing and passed it on. This is the best-case scenario. They had solid financial habits, they led by example, and they educated you along the way. In addition, they cut you off when they should have. They also saved money for you, taught you how to save money, and showed you exactly what to do with it.
2. They knew what they were doing but didn't bother or didn't have the time (for whatever reason) to teach you any of it. This is a pretty rare scenario, but definitely one worth mentioning.
3. They had no clue how to manage money properly, and they set a bad financial example for you. You still love them. They still love you. We aren't voting them off the island. We're just agreeing they didn't teach you many good financial habits.
4. They had no clue what they were doing, but they thought they did. This is a flat-out dangerous situation for everyone. If you inherited a get-rich-quick mentality, a "blame other people for your financial problems" mentality, or a "game the bankruptcy laws" mentality, then we have some serious work to do.

Not only do you need to learn how to budget, but how, in some cases, to reverse years of financial socialization. It's time to face the facts of your financial upbringing. Bluntly, it may have sucked. That's okay. But that doesn't mean that you have to perpetuate the suckiness of the past. Stand up for your present. Stand up for your future.

And even more is at stake. If you are a parent, your children may already be picking up some of these bad habits. Your problem may have become multi-generational. Therefore, as you sharpen your skills as an adult, realize that your own children are watching you now–and they're making mental notes.

If you have a bad relationship with money, then your children will have a bad relationship with money. If you give your kids all the luxuries in life–but don't show them that luxuries come through hard work and wise investing–then they won't understand the value of a dollar.

THE SKILLS

Naturally, you are wondering exactly what skills you need in order to thrive. What skills did your parents teach you–or fail to teach you? To get those answers, you need to do just one thing: purchase my next book. (Just kidding–I'm about to reveal them to you.)

You need to master four basic money skills in order to more-effectively budget. They are:
1. Understanding cash flow.
2. Using cash responsibly.
3. Using a debit card responsibly.
4. Knowing how to handle credit cards and debt.

Let's take a look at each of these skills in more detail.

1. UNDERSTANDING CASH FLOW

This is the most important concept. Cash flow allows you to accomplish everything you want in life–as long as you treat it right. People often neglect their cash flow when they make financial decisions. Your goal should be to constantly increase your cash flow.

What is your cash flow?

Cash flow literally describes the flow of money into your household (income) and the flow of money out of your household (expenses). A *positive* net cash flow means you have more money coming in than going out, and a *negative net* cash flow means you have more money going out than coming in. These net cash flows are also known, respectively, as a surplus and a shortage. We will discuss these at greater length later in the book.

You'll never know for sure what's going on with your money unless you track it. Controlling your cash flow is the single most financially responsible thing you can do. When people say you need to learn to walk before you learn to run, they are describing this very concept. Understanding cash flow is a fundamental financial baby step, yet it's the one thing people gleefully ignore.

Often, the more money you make, the more you ignore cash-flow management. When you feel broke, you usually do something about it (i.e., monitor your cash flow). But when you feel abundant, you may not feel as concerned about where your money goes. This principle is what typically prevents people who have increased their income from increasing their wealth.

In addition, it's important that you don't keep too much money at your disposal. Whether intentionally or accidentally, many people experience manufactured financial tranquility as a result of keeping too much money in their checking accounts. While this may sound like a good problem to have, it is dangerous. A checking account has a very low yield, meaning your money only gains a minimal amount of interest when it instead could be working for you. But more importantly, and less obviously, it can ruin an otherwise perfectly good financial situation.

Let me explain by using my favorite bathroom resource–toilet paper–as an example. As unpleasant as it is to think about, we've all been faced with the very alarming prospect of being stranded without the appropriate amount of toilet paper. It may sound humorous now, but it's extremely unfunny in the moment. The point is, faced with the cardboard, you will survive in any way possible, and you'll learn two lessons because of it: 1) Check supply levels before you use the bathroom!, and 2) Be resourceful. It's easy to be wasteful when you have a full roll and you forget what you went through when faced with an empty roll.

The same thing can happen when you have a relatively large roll, er, balance in your checking account. This feeling of financial abundance can occur with as little as $100 or $200 "extra" in your checking account. The amount of money that causes this strangely damaging phenomenon is different for everyone. It all depends at what amount you start to be relatively complacent.

Think about your checking account. At what point do you stop checking the balance in your head (or online) before making a purchase? When you have a cushion of $100? $200? $500? When you become comfortable with your cushion, your economic stress eases, and you start making spending decisions that aren't always prudent or even practical. This is what I like to call "abundance spending" and it can manifest itself in several ways. A feeling of financial comfort can lead you to buy items normally out of your price range for one very simple reason: you know you presently have the money to cover them. The larger the cushion you give yourself, the larger the financial mistakes you can make. For example, think about all of the celebrities and once-well-off public figures who have gone bankrupt. When you hear these stories, you wonder how someone who once had so much could now have next to nothing. I'm not a betting man (but you probably already knew that), but I'd guess that in 99% of these cases, abundance mentality played a very large role.

But back to the concept of cash flow. There are two ways you can increase yours:

1. Spend less money by controlling your expenses.
2. Make more money.

Despite popular belief, more money is not always the solution to your financial problems. When you give an undisciplined person more money, he or she is likely to end up in financial trouble again. The solution to what ills you is not more money–it's spending less. So if you want to improve your monthly cash flow, start by cutting your expenses. Otherwise, you are filling your money bucket with more money...despite the fact that there is a hole in the bucket. We will take a more comprehensive look at reducing your spending in Chapter 3.

2. USING YOUR CASH RESPONSIBLY (AND AVOIDING BLISSFUL IGNORANCE)

The proper use of cash is a skill. If you handle it correctly, you can greatly improve your financial situation. But if you treat your cash like Monopoly money, you'll end up mortgaging all of your properties and throwing the thimble, top hat, or race car across the room.

It is harder to track your spending if you use cash. (That is the essence of money laundering, but that's another book altogether.) If you are serious about increasing your net cash flow, then don't fall victim to blissful ignorance.

The misappropriation of cash in the corporate world leads to many white-collar crime convictions. The misappropriation of cash in your household leads to irresponsible financial management and falling short of your financial goals.

Often, people use cash so that someone else (a spouse) doesn't know what they spend their money on. (I'm not even talking about the men who not only prefer cash but have a penchant for one-dollar bills, in particular. That topic will not be covered in this book.) I have told many husbands they need to stop withdrawing cash to improve their cash flow. I can tell by the look in their eyes that they don't want anyone to know what they spend money on. That doesn't necessarily mean they're doing anything wrong. Rather, some people just don't like to be held accountable for their spending. In the corporate world, there's a name for people like this: embezzlers. And later on, instead of spending cash haphazardly, they're trading smokes to their cellmate Fat Tony for protection in the big house.

Cash income should be viewed the same way as cash spending. Many workers in the service industry who receive cash gratuities rarely want that income to be accounted for. There is a term for that, too: tax evasion.

Cash can be a great financial tool when used properly. In fact, you can actually spend less money when you limit yourself to cash–even during the holidays. It's simple. Predetermine in September how much you *can* spend on gifts for the December holiday season. Once you have set your total December holiday gift budget, divide that number by four. Next, in each of those four months leading up to the holidays (e.g., September, October, and November, December), take out cash and place it in an envelope. Then, as the holidays near, take money from the envelope and pay for gifts entirely with cash.

The glory of this technique comes in two forms. First, your spending can't get out of control *if* you allow yourself to spend only the money in the envelope. Best of all, you won't have the holiday blues when the credit card statement arrives in January. It is very difficult to get motivated to have a great financial year when you are paying for the mistakes of the prior year.

Many people turn to this old-school method (maybe even the one your grandparents used) for managing their entire household budget. The envelope method of budgeting is time-tested and foolproof (as we discussed briefly above). Well, unless you act foolish and spiral out of control. The envelope method involves cashing your paycheck and putting the cash into various envelopes, and then using these envelopes to pay different bills: utilities, groceries, and even savings. The envelope method isn't for everyone because it takes an incredible amount of discipline and teamwork. In addition, the envelope can pose a bit of a personal security risk. It can be nerve-racking to walk around with envelopes full of cash. No matter how much cash you choose to carry, be sure to manage it responsibly. Don't lose site of the fact that you need to account for whatever money you spend, in any form that you spend it.

3. DEALING WITH A DEBIT CARD (A.K.A. "THE IGNORANCE ENABLER")

There once was a time when people balanced their checkbooks. It was called the 1980s. Just picture it ... A young couple is sitting at the dining room table listening to Wham! and eating Steak-umms. They're wearing leg-warmers, paying bills, and balancing the checkbook.

Back then, there were fewer ways to make a financial transaction. Your options were cash, check, and charge. You received your canceled checks in the mail, so you knew when your party was paid. It's no wonder our parents have struggled to teach us how to manage money in the twenty-first century. The reality is that we would actually be in a better place if we still balanced our checkbooks, but most people don't. Technology has created convenience, and this convenience has created a new type of ignorance.

Two convenient yet overused items emerged in the 1990s: the fanny pack and the debit card. While the fanny pack certainly is convenient, its insistence that you store things much in the way a marsupial would, leaves me wanting more out of my containment solutions. The debit card is the height of convenience. If you don't have cash, you can put a purchase on the plastic, and it's automatically withdrawn from your checking account. You don't need to carry around a checkbook, and more than one account holder can use the cards at the same time, in two different locations. You would think the only prerequisite would be having money in your checking account to cover the purchases. Alas, this isn't the case, because that would make too much sense. Why would a bank offer you convenience if it doesn't improve its bottom line? It generally wouldn't. Banks make billions of dollars every year on debit card fees.

Fast-food restaurants accept debit cards, car washes accept debit cards, and even the telephone company accepts debit cards. Thanks to the debit card, the critical thinking that used to guide our financial decision-making has decreased, while our number of financial transactions has increased.

Think about how easy it is to let your life be dictated by your debit card. The convenience of the card often overshadows the problems it can create.

Here's how a day can go terribly wrong, thanks to your debit card: You wake up in the morning and head to work. Stopping at Starbucks, you buy a coffee for $185, err, $ 1.85 with your debit card. Once at the office, you purchase some Girl Scout cookies from a co-worker's daughter; the $9 charge also goes on your debit card. You go to your favorite deli for lunch and spend $8.56 on your debit card. On the way back to the office, you stop to buy a birthday card for your Aunt Helen: $3.56 on your debit card. You then make travel arrangements for your vacation, putting $1,235.86 on your debit card. On your way home from work, you pick up dry cleaning for $21.74 on your debit card. You then stop and get a pizza for the family for $15.87–another debit.

In just twelve hours' time, you have made seven transactions and spent $1,287.44. You may have the receipts in your pocket, but will you save them at the end of the day? Did you reconcile your check register? Did you accidentally overdraft and get hit with seven different overdraft charges? If you average three transactions a day for a month, are you going to keep track of ninety-three transactions as they relate to your monthly budget?

Misusing your debit cards (and make no mistake about it, this is misuse) is the same as misusing cash. But when you run out of cash, you stop spending it. At times, a debit card can be just as bad as a credit card, but instead of paying interest, you are paying pricey overdraft fees.

What's the solution? Make a commitment to discipline. If you are going to enjoy the convenience of a debit card, you should be willing to track every purchase against your budget on a monthly basis. It is nearly impossible to keep a mental note on more than ninety transactions during the course of a month.

On top of the problems you create for yourself via frequent debt card use, your bank can create problems for you as well. As of 2012, many financial institutions have started increasing the fees associated with debit card accounts. In many instances, these institutions are charging between $.75-$1.50 every time you enter your debit card PIN (Personal Identification Number). This means every time that you withdraw money out of the ATM or every time you enter your PIN to purchase something at a store, you are a creating a fee. You can easily rack up $50 per month in these silly fees if you have a debit card usage-frequency issue.

4. KNOWING HOW TO HANDLE CREDIT CARDS

Have you noticed the phrase "We can't afford it" has vanished from the English language? People today have blurred the line between what they can and cannot afford.

For people who are already financially disciplined, credit cards can be an effective tool. But if you are not disciplined–if you don't have an emergency fund and if you literally don't have the assets to cover the proposed liability–then you can't afford it. It's really that easy. Let me explain why.

Accidents happen. Sometimes you are forced to spend money when you don't expect to. Medical emergencies occur, car brakes fail, and dogs get sick. Each of these can happen suddenly and may require the use of emergency funds. Hopefully you have emergency funds, because if you don't, you will have no choice but to use your credit card.

Let's look at a rather common situation. You take your dog, Mr. Belvedere, to the vet for his annual checkup. You are already prepared for the normal costs this incurs. The charges include a $37 exam fee, $7 to weigh the dog, $13 to take a fecal sample, and $11 to throw away the fecal sample. (Tangent alert: ironically, if Mr. Belvedere leaves his own stool sample in the vet's lobby, the receptionist cleans it up for free. But inside the exam room, they steal the fecal sample from his backside so they can charge you more money.) Anyway, the vet discovers that Mr. Belvedere needs a new spleen. You are in tears. Mr. Belvedere has been your dog for six years! He watches football with you on Sundays, snores when he sleeps, and really is your best friend. Plus, you know nothing about spleens other than you're pretty sure they're slimy... and expensive. The vet tells you he can find a new spleen for Mr. Belvedere–at a cost of $5,000.

AAAAAUUUGGHHHH.

Fortunately, you have your credit card to pay for this emergency and you can curb your spending over the next year to account for the problem.

Let's compare this situation to another common scenario. It's a Sunday morning, and you awake to the sound of Mr. Belvedere and his new spleen barking. You decide to get up and check on him. It turns out he's just barking at his reflection in the stainless-steel refrigerator. You love that fridge. It came with the house, and you're just waiting for the dishwasher and stove to break so you can get stainless-steel appliances to match your glorious, gleaming fridge.

You stroll outside to get the Sunday morning paper, and you start looking through the six-inch stack of circulars. You scour an electronics-superstore ad to check the price on the new album everybody's buzzing about. The store doesn't list the CD–but something else catches your eye. You can't believe what you're seeing. The store has a sale on all stainless-steel appliances, and it turns out the more you buy, the bigger your discount!

You're quickly brought back to reality when you realize something major: you have no money set aside for any major purchases. But you decide to go to the store anyway...just to see how shiny the appliances look in person. When you get there, you're greeted by Glen, the salesman of the month (his glossy eight-by-ten photo grins at you from the Wall of Fame). You, of course, are no match for Glen's superior sales training–and you end up buying a new stove, dishwasher, and microwave. You put your purchases on the store credit card (because you save an extra ten percent), and that way you can pay off the balance over the next year or so. It's only $5,000, after all.

This is a classic example of poor budget planning.

PAYING YOUR CREDIT CARD OFF AT THE END OF THE MONTH ISN'T GOOD ENOUGH

I'm not a proponent of using your credit card to fund all purchases, and then paying it off at the end of the month. There is a giant group of people that swear by this method, but I feel they are misguided and haven't thought the process all the way through. Of all the groups of people that I encounter, the "charge everything and pay it off at the end of the month in order to get credit card rewards and cash back offers" group is far and away the most overconfident. And what the last 13 years has taught me is that overconfidence leads to financial mistakes.

I encounter at least 10 people per week via email, Twitter, or Facebook who want to argue the "charge everything and pay it off at the end of the month" method with me. They tell me about all the rewards they get, they tell me how they pay for Christmas gifts with the rewards points they receive, and they go into great detail about how committed they are to paying off their entire balance at the end of each month. But what they don't realize is their logic has failed them. The discipline that's required to pay off a card at the end of every month opens them to a lack of financial accountability throughout the month. Their commitment to pay off their debt at the end of each month, no matter how much it is, is exactly what gets them in trouble. Here are the reasons why:

1.
YOU RARELY CHECK YOUR CREDIT CARD BALANCE MID-MONTH.

People who do most of their spending with their checking accounts generally check their account balances at least twice (most likely 10 times) per month. While monitoring your checking account balance isn't exactly the perfect way to watch your spending, it's a helluva lot better than never checking your balance, especially if you are trying to live lean and cut spending. People who charge everything and then worry about it later (the end of the month), don't really care how much they spent mid-month because they aren't in danger of insufficient funds. The "charge everything and pay it off at the end of the month" people never approach their credit card limit during the course of the month. This means that spending habits gone awry will not be addressed until the behavior has passed. This isn't good. Your spending habits should be studied. How do you study them? By monitoring your spending. Have you ever had one of those weeks where stress, a sense of abundance, or the commerce fairy has caused you to spend money like it was going out of style? Join the club. Everyone has. But when you "charge everything and pay it off at the end of the month," you tend to ignore this problem until the bill cycle is over. No one ever goes on a three day spending bender, and then checks his or her credit card balance mid-billing cycle.

2.
YOUR SPENDING IS MUCH LESS CONSISTENT.

Scarcity is one of the best financial tools on the planet. I personally use it all the time to accomplish very important personal financial goals. However, when you exclusively use your credit card to buy things, then you kick scarcity out of the equation. What's your credit card limit? $15,000 or so? That's about typical for someone that uses the "charge everything and pay it off at the end of the month" method. For the sake of conversation, let's say that you put $4000 per month on your credit card. Since you plan on paying your credit card bill off at the end of the month, then you have at least $4000 in your account. Right? And what is even more likely is that you have approximately $10,000 in your checking account prior to paying your mortgage and credit card bill. How do I know this? Because about 40% of your spending is discretionary spending. You know, the type of spending that you put on your credit card. My point? Between your swollen checking account and your $15,000 credit limit, you have "access" to $25,000 per month. This is a drain on anyone's self control. You can afford ANYTHING you want. It is my experience, both as an individual consumer and as an expert, that this is a very, very bad thing. Right now you might be thinking, "No way, Pete. I've never even considered that I have access to $25,000." Yes, you have. Your brain has. Let's say that you go to your grandma's house for Thanksgiving dinner, and she has a bowl of M&Ms out for everyone to enjoy. In the first scenario, she has one four ounce bag of M&Ms in a small dish for your entire family to pick at through the course of the day. How do most people address this situation? They simply pick up just a few M&Ms with their finger tips. In the second scenario, grandma went to Costco. She has an entire three gallon punch bowl filled with M&Ms. How do most people deal with this scenario? They jam their fists so far into the bowl that it looks like they are trying to rehab a shoulder injury. The large punch bowl filled with M&Ms will result in more consumption EVERY SINGLE

TIME. Yet, your hunger never changed. Nothing changed except your snap judgement on the resources made available to you. Scarcity will help you accomplish financial goals much more than abundance will.

3.
YOU THINK YOU'RE BEATING THE SYSTEM.

Much like the guy that has a "system" for winning consistently at roulette, "charge everything and pay it off at the end of the month" people tend to think they are smarter than the house. The house ALWAYS wins. Do you really think these multi-billion dollar companies with their marketing and consumer behavior research departments are really giving you free stuff? Oh, come on. They are counting on you overspending, or better yet, they are waiting for your commitment to pay off your balance every month to fade. When it fades, then the interest clock starts. And don't think the credit card companies don't make money off of you if you pay off your balance. They have other revenue streams attached to your purchases such as swipe fees. In my opinion, you can't win.

Credit card problems generally begin with failed logic. Even people who feel like they are beating the system suffer from failed logic. Here are two very common examples of failed logic.

FAILED LOGIC #1:

I GET 1% CASH BACK ON PURCHASES, HOW IS THAT BAD?

Many credit card companies now offer you cash back on your purchases. This means you receive somewhere between 1-3% of what you charge on the card, in the form of a bill credit or check from the credit card company. This is much less exciting than it seems. How much money do you spend each month on your credit card? $2500? $3500? Let's say that you put $2500 per month on your credit card. What is 1% of $2500? $25. Wow, that's amazing. You received 25 whole American dollars for risking so much more. What are the chances that you overspend by over 1% each month on your credit card? I would say that chances are about 100%. As we discussed earlier, access to copious amounts of money is a bad thing when it comes to controlling spending. I believe people who employ the "charge everything and pay it off at the end of the month" method overspend by at least 10% per month. This means that your 1% or even 3% cash back sucks. It sucks really bad. You are actually negative between 7-9% per month.

FAILED LOGIC #2:

I MAKE ENOUGH MONEY AND SPEND ENOUGH MONEY TO MAKE THE REWARDS WORTH IT.

Okay Patrick Ewing, great job. Once again, high income doesn't necessarily mean you are a financial genius. It just means you make a lot of money. So, in your mind you immediately said to yourself, "I spend much more that $2500 on my credit card. I spend closer to $10,000 per month on my card." The percentages didn't change. Your cash back "reward" would be $100 per month, and your likely amount of financial waste would be $1,000 per month. You can't spend your way out of trouble.

A FEW ADDITIONAL NOTES ON CREDIT CARDS

Store credit card problems can be avoided quite simply.

Let's talk about luge, for a second. Luge is one of the most dangerous sports in the world. You are almost guaranteed an injury if you participate in this spectacular sport. I have never been injured in a luge accident. Why? Because I have never luged. Do you want to know how to avoid problems with store credit cards? Don't ever get one.

A NOTE ABOUT CREDIT CARDS AS A BACKUP PLAN

The common denial that things can and will go wrong is often the catalyst of a financial disaster. Life happens. And life generally costs money. Tires lose their tread, pets get sick, and basements sometimes flood. You need to have a plan in place to deal with these "unexpected expenses" (although they aren't really that unexpected). Poor contingency plans plague my generation. If my fellow Gen Yers actually do have an emergency money plan, then it usually is built with what I call

"Financial Paper Mache." This means the backup plan appears to be solid, but it's actually pretty weak. The most common backup plans for Gen Y (and other generations) are:

1. Parents bailing you out
2. Going into debt on your credit card

A few years ago I was having lunch with a good friend, and was lucky enough to be sitting next to a disaster in action. A 30 year-old(ish) woman was talking her 60 year-old(ish) father into paying off her car and her credit cards. The woman's financial backup plan, credit, was being bailed out by her other financial backup plan, her father. This story will end terribly. If you are anywhere near 30 years old, and you still consider asking your parents for money, then please allow these words to be your wake-up call. The later in life you drink from the money teat of your parents, the harder it will be to go without their assistance. Borrowing (which often turns into a gift, although people are too wussy to admit it) from your parents is the absolute worst backup plan you can conceive. You must eliminate the infancy of this thought from your head. Selling your foot to raise money would be a better idea (I'm only half-kidding). How many times have you said to yourself, "I have a credit card in case of emergencies"? My guess is you have said it frequently, and you have even been somewhat self-congratulatory in this proclamation. Besides, being debt free and having a credit card for the sole purpose of handing an emergency seems like a brilliant plan. I used to feel this way. But then I realized that by having my credit card be my backup plan I was actually becoming complacent. If you have $10,000 (credit available on your card) at your immediate disposal, are you likely to push yourself to save $10,000 in cash money? No. This is where I will argue to the death with the industry phrase "responsible use of credit." A zero balance card, used as a major backup plan, will actually hold most people back financially. This is NOT a responsible use of credit. This credit is damaging your financial future. I see it everyday. If you have had trouble accumulating assets, even with a zero balance on your credit card, then this credit card complacency may be to blame.

There is an alternative to these two terrible backup plans. Money. What's that, you ask? It's what people used to use to buy things or fund emergency spending. Our government used to use it, our grandparents used to use it, and our employers used to use it. Money trumps credit. My financial backup plan is funded with money, my money (and by my money, I mean our money (Mrs. Planner and me)). Is it hard to accumulate money? Yes. But believe it or not, it's actually easier to accumulate money when you don't have another poor backup plan in your way. Examine your backup plan. You may be surprised to learn that this previously considered prudent plan actually is holding you back financially. One more thing. Please, please, please eliminate the "possibility" of borrowing money from your parents. No matter what your financial situation is right now, it will be worsened in the long term if you borrow money from your parents. And yes, borrowing is the same damn thing as accepting a gift.

These four concepts—understanding cash flow, using your cash responsibly, dealing with a debit card, and knowing how to handle credit cards—will make or break you. Mastering them takes practice and discipline. But beware. If you ignore even one of them, you are still in trouble.

These concepts are financial survival tips. You wouldn't go camping without an air mattress, space heater, and satellite dish, would you? (I mean, you wouldn't go without a compass.) Well, you can't survive financially without mastering these four concepts.

CHAPTER THREE

REDUCING SPENDING AND UNDERSTANDING THE NEW NECESSITIES

SOME PEOPLE MAY DEFINE FINANCIAL PROGRESS AS "BEING ABLE TO AFFORD MORE."

I DEFINE IT DIFFERENTLY: "NEEDING LESS MONEY TO LIVE."

The fewer financial obligations you have, the more freedom you have. Yet, in part due to the influence of marketing and the media, Americans tend to add obligations as they increase their income and their wealth. If you measure your success by what you have, you are in deep trouble. This isn't cause for panic, though, because you can adjust this attitude. Your spending habits, no matter how deeply seated they are, can change. They must change, especially if they are the roadblocks standing in the way of your financial progress.

Not only do you need to change your current "fixed" spending habits, but you must also reduce the number of financial obligations you have and continue to accept. By making some subtle changes that will have a major impact on your bottom line, you can easily reclaim thousands of dollars per year from your budget.

The following four spending categories can immediately reflect your growing financial awareness (or lack thereof).

1. Groceries
2. Dining out
3. Utilities
4. The New Necessities

GROCERIES

The grocery store is a microcosm of your world when it comes to spending decisions. In this microcosm, you can isolate certain behaviors and decision-making processes, analyze them, and then use the resulting data to alter your financial behaviors in all spending situations. Do you make impulsive purchases or stick to your grocery list? Are you easily distracted by shiny and sparkly items? These are the type of questions you will consider when analyzing your grocery-store habits. Good decisions at the grocery store can benefit you in two ways.

1. They can directly and positively affect your finances in specific areas of your life:

- By planning meals based on what's on sale and in season, you can reduce your impulse buying, overspending, and food waste. Buying in season and local reduces food transportation costs, thus reducing your cost.
- You can decrease your health-care costs by making proper food choices.
- If you can become immune to catchy, but often meaningless, grocery-store marketing tactics (such as flashy packaging and strategic shelf placement), you can apply the same discretion to other such tactics that appeal more to your senses than to your needs.

2. They can help you develop the following good habits, which will carry over to all financial decisions:

- Frugality
- Willpower
- Strategic planning and execution of your plan
- Prioritizing
- Budgeting and problem solving

If it seems like I'm putting a lot of pressure on your trip to the grocery store, that's because I am. Whereas you've no doubt come to consider these trips a means of picking up food for dinner, I'm focused on the part they play in a much grander financial plan. Think about it. When you walk through a grocery store, one particular concept is abundantly clear: choice. You could buy anything you want, but should you? You could look for deals, but will your desire for instant gratification trump your need for a good bargain? You could buy brand names, but generic is cheaper and not very different (if at all) from brand-name items. You get to choose how much your compulsions will cost you, and how much money you need for instant gratification.

DINING OUT

Not only is dining out convenient, it's fun. No shopping for hard-to-find ingredients, no lengthy preparation, and perhaps best of all, no clean-up.

Unfortunately, if you don't have a grasp on how dining out affects your financial life, you could be in for a great deal of trouble long after you pay the bill.

Sixty-six percent of American adults say they dine in a restaurant at least once a week. A statistic like this one no doubt results, in large part, from our hectic work schedules. If you're a member of the great American rat race like I am, sometimes you simply don't have the time or the energy to go grocery shopping and prepare adequate meals. On the other hand, if you're working incredibly long hours to sustain your indulgent dining habits, then you might be in the middle of a nasty cycle. (If you're just a workaholic, that's a completely different issue altogether.) Yet to many, dining out is not only a source of sustenance, it's a primary source of entertainment. Both of these situations are common and fair. But no matter how you look at it, you should be fully aware of how dining out affects your personal bottom line.

The absolute best way to curb your spending on dining out is to track it on a weekly basis. This means giving yourself a weekly dining out budget. Whether it's $75 or $20, it's much easier to keep track of the 21 meals in a week, than the 93 meals in a month.

UTILITIES

The same discipline you develop in other areas of your financial life can be applied to reducing your utility expenses. The average American has upwards of six or seven fixed expenses each month, including utility bills. But how much attention do you give your utility bills each month?

If you're like most Americans, probably not much. We tend to take the cost of "fixed" bills like these for granted. But are utility bills really fixed? Not really. Your habits, knowledge, and overall awareness can affect them, and you can reduce your utility costs with very little effort. So what do you say? Would you tweak a couple of your habits if it meant freeing up $300 per year? I thought you would.

Take the time to explore the various money-saving programs your different utility providers offer (but which they may not always go out of their way to advertise). For instance, can you bundle your different services? Can you switch to budget billing to avoid seasonal spikes on your bill?

Familiarize yourself with your utility providers' different payment options, either by calling the companies or visiting their websites. Compare those options to the amount you pay monthly. Are you spending more than you need to in order to get the services you need? If so, make changes, if that will ultimately save you money, and then watch the savings happen over the next few months.

You need to manage your utility bills in the same way you manage your assets. Since changing your financial life is all about changing your habits, adopt the following money-saving and energy-saving habits:

1. Consider installing a programmable thermostat. This allows you to be energy efficient when you're away from your home during the day. If you don't have a programmable thermostat, settle on a temperature a few degrees lower (during winter) and higher (during summer) than you're used to. You'll be surprised by how much you can save.

2. Turn off your lights when you leave a room. This is such an easy and obvious way to conserve energy and save money—yet few people do it. There's no need to keep lights on in unoccupied rooms, nor is there really a reason to light your front lawn or backyard at night. If you're concerned about intruders or safety, consider switching to motion-detecting lights, which can lead to significant savings over time.

3. Conserve water. Even if your water company doesn't offer an incentive to adopt water-conserving strategies, the potential savings should be incentive enough. Switching to low-flow shower heads and aerated faucets and adding "float boosters" to your toilet tank are great ways for homeowners to lower their water bills.

4. Unplug appliances and other devices that use energy when not in use. This includes your television, toaster, cell-phone charger, and your hair dryer. Also, turn off surge protectors and power strips when you're not using the electronics plugged into them. Keeping these items plugged in wastes energy and money.

5. Evaluate your need for a home phone. Sometimes a cell phone can replace a traditional one entirely. Many people no longer need a land line but keep it because they don't want to get rid of a phone number they've had for years. But paying the phone company a fixed amount every month simply for the privilege of having a sentimental phone number and a service you can live without is a lot more painful than the steps you can take to replace your home phone with your cell phone once and for all. If you already have a cell phone and are ready to make the switch, start by emailing your contacts your new number. Next, put your cell-phone number on your land-line voicemail or answering machine for a month prior to turning off your home phone service. Finally, personally call those whom you want to have your new number (and skip those whom you don't!).

6.   Check for air leaks around windows and doors; seal cracks and drafty spaces. Why spend time and money heating or air conditioning your home if the air is escaping? The principle of preventing waste alone should motivate you to investigate your home's efficiency. The principle of saving money is icing on the cake.

These steps may seem minor, but the small things truly do have the largest effects. In my experience, making these changes can save you as much as $300 per year, which you can put toward real financial priorities.

My client Gabe's story clearly illustrates how these tactics can save money. Gabe, a school counselor and summertime landscaper, always had budgeting problems. During the winter, his problem was particularly pronounced: heating costs were stretching his paycheck so thin that he was constantly hit with overdraft charges. Because one of his jobs is seasonal, his income is higher during the summer (and his heating bills are obviously lower as well.). So his real issue wasn't budgeting, but timing–and awareness. When I sat down with him, he admitted he had never taken the time to consider how his utility bills could be affected by his habits and decisions–he had just come to accept winter high heating bills as a fact of life.

The solution? At my urging, he took five minutes to contact his natural gas provider and signed up for their budget-billing program. The program, which spreads heating costs over the entire year's bills, allowed him to pay a consistent amount each month. Instead of having his bill fluctuate between $50 and $400 each month, depending on the season, he now pays a fixed fee of $150 per month. This fixed bill didn't eliminate any of Gabe's debt per se, but it did make it easier for him to budget year-round, which drastically improved his ability to focus on his financial goals and the other areas of his budget that needed attention.

THE NEW NECESSITIES

Without a real grasp of their traditional costs (like utilities)–the majority of Americans have begun justifying the addition of new fixed expenses as well. I'm not going to make the case for getting rid of things you consider necessities–although you should certainly consider it if you're in debt–but they can add up and drain your checking account if each expense isn't monitored intently. Perhaps the first question you should ask yourself is whether or not all of your necessities are, in fact, necessities.

Chances are, you now have a greater number of "basic life necessities" than you did ten or twenty years ago–and your list of basic "needs" is probably drastically larger than that of your parents. This is due to what I call the "Simplicity-Needs Paradox," the contradiction presented when, in taking steps to simplify your life by decreasing the amount of energy you expend on routine tasks, you increase the number of basic needs necessary to maintain your new level of simplicity.

For example, email is far faster than snail mail, but in order to have access to email, you have to have a computer. Thus, in order to simplify, you have to acquire. As you simplify your financial life, you'll have to account for the New Necessities that have become basic needs. But with so many New Necessities, how are you ever going to free up enough money to start saving? The basic fact of the matter is, you can't start saving until you stop spending. Easier said than done, right? The following "The New Necessities Exercise" will help you take a bite out of unnecessary spending while still keeping up with the Joneses (or at least with basic culturally current needs). Fill out the questions on the next page, and you'll likely find that you can free up at least $70 per month.

How much do you spend on the following? (PART ONE)

- Internet access
- Cable/internet
- Coffee/tobacco addiction
- Music
- Lunch out
- Cell phone

WHERE CAN YOU CUT BACK? (PART TWO)

Do you really need the fastest Internet service available? Is there a cheaper plan? Is there a way to consolidate the services you now get into one lower monthly plan? Assuming I'm not driving you back into the Dark Ages of dial-up, which I wouldn't wish upon anyone, write down the potential monthly savings.

$ _ _ _ _ _ _

Do you even watch your premium cable channels? I didn't, so I opted for the lesser package. You might also be able to unsubscribe from certain channels à la carte, which can also reduce your monthly costs. What does the package one tier below yours cost?

$_ _ _ _ _ _

How much would you save by unsubscribing from just those premium channels you don't watch, or which you watch infrequently?

$_ _ _ _ _ _

Do you regularly buy frou-frou coffee drinks? How much would you save if you switched to normal coffee and then doctored it with milk and sugar?

$_ _ _ _ _ _

Music and movies can be an addiction, but that doesn't mean you have to buy/download them. (No, this isn't where I tell you how to how to steal it.) Instead, you can go to most libraries and get CDs and DVDs to listen to before you buy. This way you can eliminate the cost of the ones you don't like or get your fix and save your dough. Seriously consider this. Even more, consider how much it would save you.

$_ _ _ _ _ _

I like overstuffed burritos, too, but there's no reason you can't cut your lunch budget in half. Make a sandwich, keep salad fixings in the fridge at work–just keep the spending at bay. How much money per month can you take off of your lunch spending?

$_ _ _ _ _ _

How can you reduce the cost of your cell phone plan? What about the monthly text-message package, or the number of monthly minutes? Can you feasibly move to the usage plan a step below your current one? Some cell phone service companies will actually sit on the phone with you to help you create a more affordable plan. But you have to be proactive and request help–they usually don't advertise this service. How much money can you save with just a couple of small changes to your cell phone plan?

$_ _ _ _ _ _

To determine how much you could save, monthly, on the New Necessities, add up the monthly totals from the first part of the exercise. Write that number down.

_ _ _ _ _

Next, add up the prospective savings you estimated in the second part of the exercise. Write that number down.

Finally, subtract the second number above from the first total above. The resulting number is how much you could be contributing to your emergency fund each month.

When I recommend this exercise to clients, I like to tell them about another client of mine, Nadia, who committed to these steps and managed to save $190 per month. She changed her cable plan, reduced the money she spent on lunch during the work week, and analyzed her cell phone plan to identify every single area where she could save.

Nadia is a good example of somebody who was wasting a fair amount of money on things she really didn't need (but thought she needed). She didn't cancel her cable; she simply re-evaluated her viewing habits and acted accordingly. She didn't discontinue her cell phone service or even limit her usage; she just discovered that she only used 68% of the minutes she purchased each month and changed plans to take advantage of the savings that come with her level of usage. (The ratio of cell phone usage to rate plan is one that most of us could stand to lower.) And Nadia's story gets even better: she was ultimately able to put all of her newly "found" money–$2,280 per year, to be exact–toward her son's college fund!

IS IT EVER OKAY TO SPLURGE?

All of this financial restraint can build up some really strange feelings. You may be tempted to blow money.

Whereas being financially responsible can be addicting, sometimes you just want to spend money. It's important to acknowledge this desire, and learn how to deal with it. Frankly, sometimes it's okay to splurge. You just need to set some ground rules to prevent the splurge from turning into a disaster.

1. **DON'T SPLURGE IN ORDER TO MAKE YOURSELF FEEL BETTER ABOUT A BAD FINANCIAL SITUATION**- I eat because I'm sad, and I'm sad because I eat. Splurging in the midst of financial struggles is a bad idea. Because once the high wears off from the splurge, reality will be all up in your grill. A good way to splurge when you are broke is to splurge with another resource: time. Take the day to yourself. Go to a park and walk around. Go walk around the mall (but don't splurge). Just collect your thoughts, and enjoy the silence. (It's quite obvious at this point that I have a toddler, isn't it?)

2. **PLAN YOUR SPLURGES**- Yes, I know that I'm taking a bit of the fun out of it. That's just what I do. Splurge once per quarter (every three months). And better yet, plan your splurges by reducing spending in other categories heading up to the big splurge.

3. **DON'T BE A MORON**- Yep, that's the type of hard-hitting advice you can only get from Pete The Planner. Splurging on a car is a bad idea. Splurging on a timeshare is a bad idea. Splurge on dinner. Splurge on a sweater. Splurge on flowers for your wife and/or girlfriend (just don't mix up the cards).

Life isn't all about restriction. Your ability to splurge responsibly will serve you well. Yes, planning your splurge is the right thing to do. Don't make this the worst advice that I have ever given, please splurge responsibly.

CHAPTER FOUR

THE
IDEAL
BUDGET

THE MOST FREQUENTLY- ASKED QUESTION I GET ON BUDGETING IS

"HOW MUCH MONEY SHOULD I BE SPENDING ON EACH EXPENSE CATEGORY?"

It's a fair question. How much should you spend on housing, transportation, food and other costs? I will gladly answer this for you, but you should understand that the percentages start to fall apart above a certain income level.

Whereas someone who makes $70,000 per year should limit his or her monthly spending on food to $490 (12% of net income), it would be rather impractical for someone who makes $300,000 per year to spend $1,800 monthly (also 12% of net income) on food.

If your household income is above $175,000, then the percentages (provided in the chart below) are best used to prevent major spending errors. People earning $175,000 would be foolish to spend $1,420/month 15% of net income) on transportation, for example. This is where I tend to disagree with a great number of highly paid individuals. Their question is typically, "I make a ton of money, so why can't I spend a ton on my car?" My answer is simple: success isn't defined by how much you can afford. You shouldn't find ways to spend your high income. The basic necessities of life are easily affordable for those who earn high incomes. This should translate into increased savings and investing of their budget surplus, but, alas, it not always does.

Don't panic if your expenses don't look exactly like the chart below. The key to this entire exercise is to make sure that your pie actually equals 100%. Yes, you may find in doing this that you spend more money than you make. We will fix this problem by the end of this book. But here is what you need to know: if you don't spend the maximum amount in one category, you can allocate more money to another category. In other words, let's say that your household transportation costs are only 5% of your income. Then you can feel comfortable allocating the "extra" 10% to other categories. This strategy is exactly how I live the financial life that

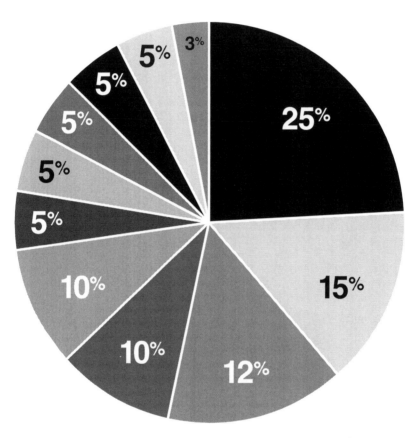

IDEAL
BUDGET

25% Housing •
15% Transportation •
12% Groceries/Dining •
10% Savings •
10% Utilities & Phone •
5% Charity •
5% Entertainment •
5% Medical •
5% Holidays/Gifts •
5% Clothing •
3% Misc •

I want to live. I have very low transportation costs; therefore, dining out and housing receive a higher portion of my income. In addition, I don't spend much on entertainment or medical care; therefore, I'm able to utilize these allocations elsewhere. See? It's kind of fun.

People who fail to operate on this "give and take" basis often find themselves in debt. Many households operate on 110% of their income. You just can't do that. You can't consistently spend more than you make and expect to come out on the other end. I encourage you to compare your household expenditures to this chart and this philosophy. What one category do you scrimp on so that you can spend more on another?

And if you are wondering about where tithing (giving 10% of your income to the church) comes into play, then this budget is based on your income after your tithe. In addition, this also excludes your 401(k) savings, which is taken out of your income prior to it being considered "take-home" pay. Thus, if you save 15% of your gross income toward your 401(k) and another 10% of your take-home pay toward general savings, you are a rock star. Check that. A rock star probably wouldn't save any money.

In order to better illustrate the ideal household budget, I'm going to focus on a hypothetical income of $70,000. That means a gross income (before taxes, benefits, retirement savings, or any other withholdings) of $70,000. However, we all spend our net income. This means I will base the hypothetical spending model on a $49,000 net income (after taxes, benefits, and retirement savings). $49,000 in monthly terms is $4,083 per month.

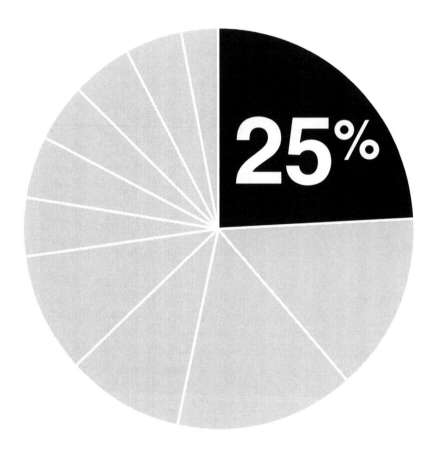

RENT/MORTGAGE (INCLUDING TAXES AND INSURANCE):

Your housing expense is generally your largest one. This means that poor decisions in regards to housing can have a long-lasting impact on your financial life.

Banks have traditionally allowed mortgage payments to approach 33% of a gross monthly income (before taxes). That's not at all surprising; a bank is in business to make money first, and help you second (or third...or fourth. Don't get me started.). Thirty-three percent of gross is very different than 25% of net. For instance, if your household income is $70,000, 33% of your gross monthly income would be $1,924 ($70,000/12=$5,833. $5,833 X 33%=$1,924). In contrast, 25% of your net income on $70,000 would be approximately $1,020 (based on $49,000 take home pay). $70,000 X 70% (30% for taxes and benefits)= $49,000 $49,000/12=$4,083 $4,083 X 25%=$1,020. That is a difference of $904 per month! I don't know about you, but I spend my net income, not my gross income.

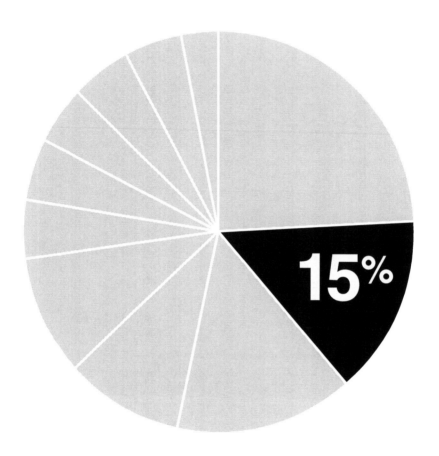

TRANSPORTATION:

Do you drive your car? Or does your car drive you ... to financial trouble? If you're fortunate enough to live in an area with good public transportation, then you're lucky.

But you are likely to face higher housing and food costs. And for the rest of us, getting to the places we need to go costs money. Historically, Americans have moved farther and farther away from our places of employment and have consistently increased the length of our car loans. You might not think so, but living twenty miles away from your job with an eight-year car loan could lead to your financial ruin.

   Transportation costs typically include car payments (leases or loans), gas, insurance, and maintenance. It is very easy to let your transportation costs creep above 15% of your take-home pay. This should lead you to one conclusion: find a semi-permanent solution to high transportation costs. Pay off your car, and settle close to your place of employment. Based on that hypothetical $70,000 income, you should allocate no more than $612 per month to transportation.

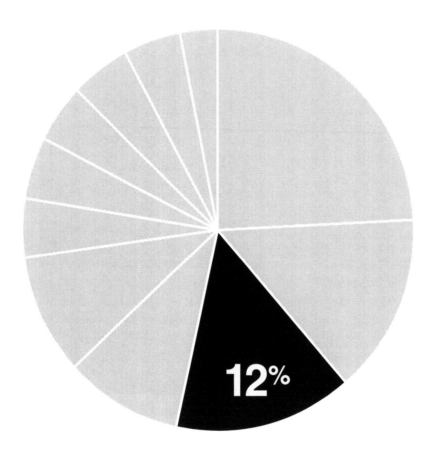

GROCERIES AND DINING OUT:

I have something terrible to say. Food is pooped. There. I said it. I'm sorry. It's unfortunate, but true.

Spending 12% of your income on something that is...err...wasted is a bad idea when you are trying to clean up your financial life. True, food is pleasure and entertainment, too. But in its simplest form, food is sustenance. Based on the hypothetical income, you should allocate no more than $490 a month to groceries and dining out.

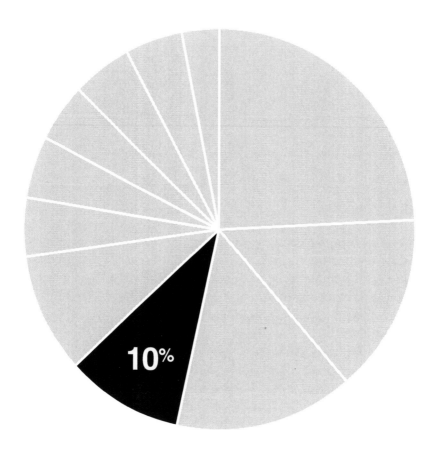

SAVINGS:

Have you ever heard the phrase "pay yourself first"? It means you should save money for the future, before allocating it to current financial needs. Your future requires that you save for it.

Not only should you save money in a company-sponsored retirement plan prior to your paycheck hitting your checking account, but you should also save 10% of your take-home pay. This isn't hard to do, if you build the habit from your first paycheck. But the further away you get from your first paycheck, the harder it gets. Based on the hypothetical income, you should save at least $408 per month in this category.

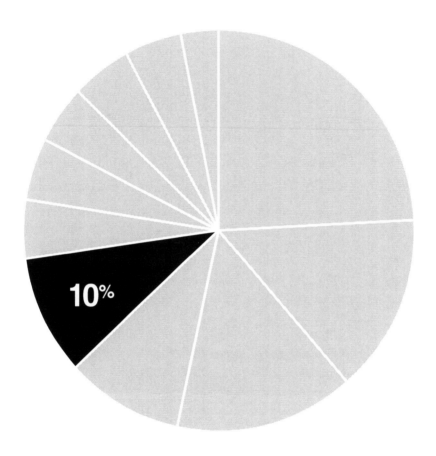

UTILITIES AND PHONE:

As we discussed previously, utilities aren't sexy. That's why so many people ignore them. But when you consider that your mobile phone, internet, and cable/satellite costs are part of this utilities category, then you start to take notice. $408 can be allocated to utilities.

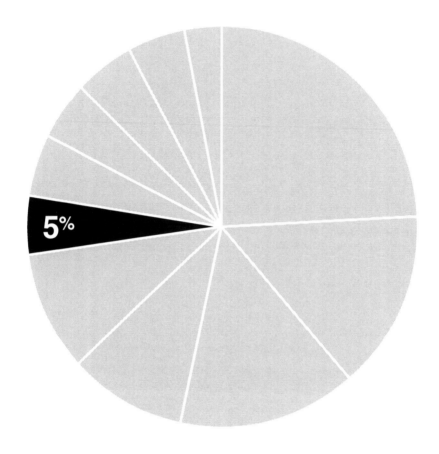

CHARITY:

When it comes to charitable giving, it's important to get into the habit as early as possible. But "giving" doesn't have to solely involve money. Plenty of people and organizations need time and resources, too.

Donating goods and volunteering are all ways of giving back, and nearly every organization is happy to have the help. Don't adopt an "I'll think of others once I take care of myself" attitude. Your needs and the needs of others can coincide. $204 should be your monthly contribution for charity.

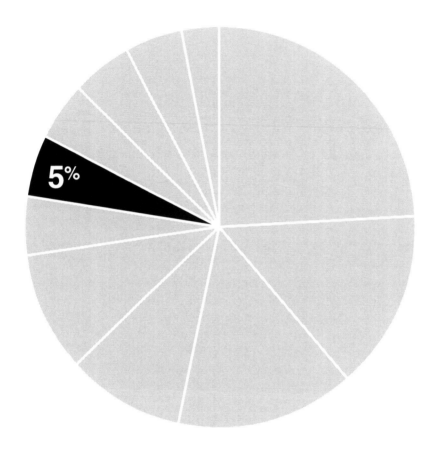

MEDICAL:

Remember, these ideal spending-percentages are based on your take-home pay. That means that if you don't have many medical expenses outside of your health insurance (which is usually pre-take-home), then you can reallocate this 5% to another category. The good news is that per our hypothetical example, you have $204 per month allocated to this category. If you don't need it, then reallocate it.

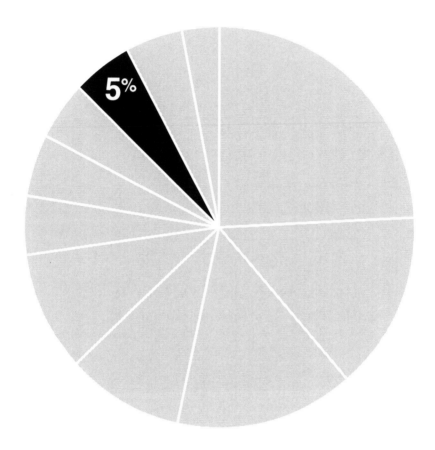

5%

CLOTHING:

What's included in the clothing budget? Everything. Clothes for you. Clothes for your kids. Clothes for your spouse. Workout clothes. Work clothes. Casual clothes. Bridesmaid dresses. Rental tuxes. Dry cleaning. Clothing repairs. Shoes. Handbags. More shoes.

You may have been excited by the raw numbers, but the "what's included" section may have brought you back to earth. Budgeting for clothing requires planning and forethought. The first step in my opinion? You MUST take care of your current clothing. You're going to need every bit of the $204 per month assigned to this category.

5%

HOLIDAYS AND GIFTS:

I have seen more people ruin their financial years in December than in any other month. Not only do they destroy their current financial year due to irresponsible spending, but they also complicate the start of the coming year.

Overspending on the holidays and on gifts (in general) is a serious problem, yet frequently rationalized as altruism. But over-gifting isn't altruism. Generosity is generally not the true motivation of over-gifters. Over-gifting is a compulsion and can lead to irreparable financial damage. I'm not trying to take the fun out of the holidays, but you need to think 60 days ahead to prevent poor holiday spending decisions. Based on the hypothetical income of $70,000, your allocation to this category should be no more than $204 per month.

PETE THE PLANNER'S HOLIDAY SAVINGS LEAGUE

The best way to fund your holiday purchases is to start setting money aside in September. I'm not talking about mentally setting money aside. I'm talking about cash money. You must withdrawal cash every month until the end of the year. That means that you are making FOUR withdrawals if you start this process in September

Place the cash in an envelope. Put the envelope in a safe place. When you go shopping for gifts this holiday season, take your envelope and use it. DO NOT GO OVER BUDGET.

The entire point of this process (which I call Pete the Planner's Holiday Savings League) is to make holiday spending easier on you. You need to establish your holiday budget right now. Take a few minutes to consider how much money you can afford to spend this coming holiday season.

Thinking through your "buy list" is the most important part of the process. By setting a spending goal now, then you are better able to set money aside for your holiday spending. If you can't afford to pre-fund your holiday spending over a period of four months, then you sure can't afford to spend that much money. See? You will make a wise budgeting decision by simply taking the time to figure out your holiday spending now. And you will do all of this without going into debt. Going into debt to pay for gifts is a really bad idea.

The best way to establish a budget is to think through your "buy list," and then set a budget for each person. For instance, 10 people @ $50 each equals $500. If this is your situation, then you should withdraw $125 in cash every month starting in September.

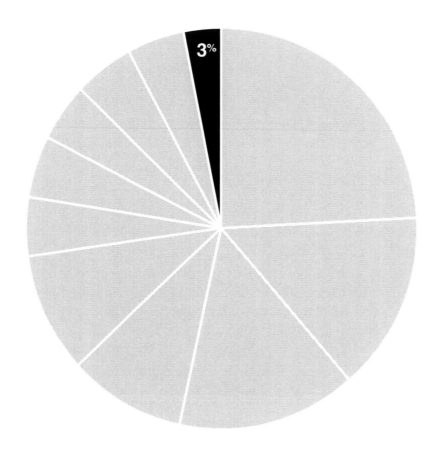

MISCELLANEOUS:

The possibilities are limitless, although you can't forget about pets, life insurance, and donkey-riding lessons. It's your money. Do what you want with it, but don't spend over $122 per month in this category.

Do you need more money for miscellaneous expenses? Then you need to reduce spending in another one of the expense categories. However, don't let your miscellaneous category get out of control. Grouping unaccounted for spending into the miscellaneous category and calling it a day isn't your aim. Account for your spending. Don't be lazy by swelling your miscellaneous expense category.

CHILD CARE REQUIRES EXTRA PLANNING

How do you account for daycare? You have to carve it out of other major areas such as transportation, dining out, gifts, and entertainment. The biggest financial mistake anyone can make is increasing spending in one area without decreasing spending in others.

There are more financial angles to the daycare question than you might think, and how to answer it is one of the toughest decisions parents can make. An incredible number of factors go into making this decision, but I'm going to limit the discussion to two primary considerations.

1. SHOULD ONE PARENT STAY HOME, OR SHOULD BOTH PARENTS WORK AND PAY FOR DAYCARE?

Let's consider the case of the average upper-middle class double in-come American household. Some people work because they want to, others work because they have to, and yet many people work because they *think* they have to. One of the most frequent financial miscalculations I see involves the "should I stay home" question. If you have ever found yourself saying, "Why am I even working? My entire check is going to daycare," then you need to take a very hard look at your budget. Many people say this, but few address it properly. If you find yourself in this position, then you probably haven't properly adjusted your budget. You *must* reduce spending in other areas drastically if you feel a majority of your income goes toward child care.

For many families, adding a child care expense can be like adding another mortgage. Here is a simple way to figure out if you should stick with two incomes, or drop down to one. Let's take a family where the second person's income is $2,200 net/month. I say "second" because I am trying to distinguish this person as the lower income-earner. Now, let's assume that daycare costs $1,100/month. How should this family think through their decision? They have two options:

    a. They can reduce their household spending by $1,100 in order to account for the new daycare expense.

    b. They can reduce their household spending by $2,200 in order to account for staying home.

There are, of course, some additional considerations such as health insurance, but in a nutshell, the above "a or b" scenario is the best way to answer this tough question, unless your child care costs too much.

2. ARE YOU LOOKING FOR THE CHEAPEST CHILD CARE OR THE BEST CHILD CARE? I hate when people say there are no wrong answers to a question. However, in this instance, I truly don't think there is a wrong answer. Assuming a certain level of quality care, the cheap option isn't necessarily a bad thing. Obviously, I don't want you to put your kid in a drawer and go to work. But don't be ashamed to accept a baseline of quality, and then seek out the most affordable option. At the same time, don't be afraid to seek out the highest-quality child care you can find, if you can afford it. Too many times we justify faulty financial decisions by invoking our children. Yes, I had that Whitney Houston album, too. I know "the children are our future" and we need to "teach them well, and let them lead the way." But it doesn't mean you have to compromise your financial future for something you could get for less. And this is exactly why I didn't put child care in the ideal household budget.

If you are a parent, then you know child care can quickly become your number one priority, but that doesn't mean you should just throw money at it. Make sure you're reducing spending in other areas so your ideal household budget doesn't take a major hit.

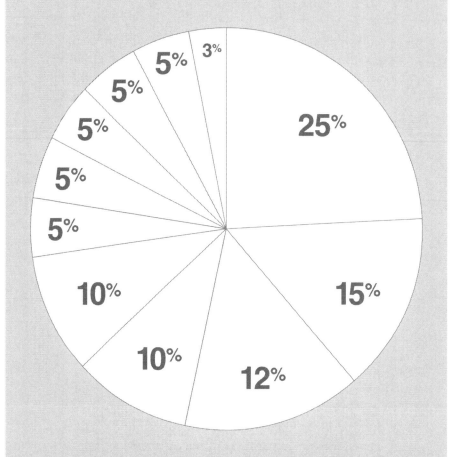

PeteThePlanner.com

WHAT YOUR DAD NEVER TAUGHT YOU ABOUT BUDGETING

IDEAL BUDGET

BUDGET CATEGORIES	RECOMMENDED PERCENTAGES	MY PERCENTAGES
Housing	25%	
Transportation	15%	
Groceries/Dining	12%	
Savings	10%	
Utilities & Phone	10%	
Charity	5%	
Entertainment	5%	
Medical	5%	
Holidays/Gifts	5%	
Clothing	5%	
Misc	3%	

CHAPTER
FIVE
COUNT YOUR TRANS- ACTIONS

DO YOU SUFFER FROM FINANCIAL NUMBNESS?

What do I mean by that? Think about habits. They're funny things. At first, we're conscious of them. Then, somehow–for good or for bad, for better or for worse–they become second nature. Under their spell, we begin to forget we've adopted them. And that's where "financial numbness" and its offshoot, "numb spending," come in.

Numb spending occurs when you're completely oblivious to the number of purchases you make. You practically live in front of the cash register–at the mall, the grocery store, the coffee shop, wherever. The problem is the more purchases you make, the less discriminating you are in your spending. It's a slippery slope from this kind of spending to overall financial numbness, which is characterized by a general indifference to understanding the details of your current finances, to tackling financial problems, or to planning for your financial future.

Fiscally smart people take all of their purchases–and their overall financial situation–quite seriously. I'm not suggesting you get into a Lincoln-Douglas debate with yourself over a pack of gum, but if you're looking to change your financial status, you've got to start thinking.

HOW MANY TIMES PER WEEK, ON AVERAGE, DO YOU MAKE A PURCHASE - AS A HOUSEHOLD?

Here's how to find out:

STEP 1: Go through your bank and credit card statements and count your purchases for the last month.

STEP 2: Gather all of the cash receipts floating around in your purse or sock drawer. You do save your receipts, right? (The near impossibility of this activity should give you a clear sense of why paying with cash is so tricky–you never really know just how many transactions you've made.)

But this doesn't mean you get to skip your cash purchases. If you can't find all (or any) of your receipts, take some serious time to think about your cash-spending habits. And if you really don't have any earthly clue as to how many transactions it takes to eat up your cash, it's probably safe to say that you have too many. Controlling the number of purchases you make will be a significant part of your success.

STEP 3: Determine your Monthly Purchase Total by adding the number of credit card and debit card purchases you gathered in Step 1 to the number of cash receipts you unearthed in Step 2. Remember, you're looking for the number of purchases you made, not the total value of these purchases. Write that number down.

_____

STEP 4: Next, divide your monthly totals by 4.33 to get your *Weekly Purchase Total.*

To determine your *Weekly Purchase Total,* divide your *Monthly Purchase Total* by 4.33 (the number of weeks in a month). (Although we're accustomed to thinking of months as having only 4 weeks (28 days), 4.33 is the more accurate number.)

Determine your Monthly Purchase Total:

Number of monthly credit card purchases   _____

Number of monthly debit card purchases   _____

Number of monthly cash purchases   _____

Monthly Purchase Total   _____

Determine your Weekly Purchase Total:

_____ / 4.33 = _____Weekly Purchase Total

STEP 5: Compare this number to the Weekly Purchases Scale below. Where do you fall?

WEEKLY PURCHASES SCALE (FOR YOUR HOUSEHOLD)

Remember: This is for both you and your significant other. Add your transactions up and measure them against the scale below.

20+ "PATHOLOGICAL PURCHASER"

You're out of control. There is simply no reason to spend money three times per day. Seriously.

15-19 "CONTINUALLY COMMERCING"

Nearly unacceptable. If you make this many transactions, chances are you often get to the end of a calendar year and wonder where all of your money went.

10-14 "MODERATELY MONEY-MINDED"

You seem to have a pretty good grasp of the importance of frugality and economic efficiency, but you have room for improvement.

5-9 "PRACTICALLY PERFECT PURCHASER"

This is pretty tough to do, but if you are serious about turning things around, five to nine weekly transactions is where you want to fall. This probably means: grocery store, gas for you, gas for your spouse, one dinner, and two lunches.

1-4 "SERIOUSLY SELECTIVE SHOPPER"

You're really broke, really boring, or really...financially awesome!

Now that you have your Weekly Purchase Total, you're ready to set your Purchase Goal. Everybody's Purchase Goal is different because everybody has a different disposable income and will be starting from a different point in his or her financial life. But for the purpose of this book, let's shoot for the stars and assume that you only want to make between five and nine transactions per week.

Reducing the number of purchases you make requires forethought and effort. It means taking lunch to work sometimes. It means you can't always go out to dinner on a whim. It means you need to start solving problems with something other than a piece of plastic. If you've determined that you have purchase "issues" (fifteen or more purchases per week), you've most likely been meeting everyday needs–eating, transportation, etc.–by making spontaneous purchases.

Reducing your spending might also require willpower or, in more extreme cases, outside intervention and assistance. For the Pathological Purchaser, purchases are a way of solving an immediate need or problem. But there's another kind of Pathological Purchaser.

This second type of Pathological Purchaser has anything from a habit to a genuine addiction for satisfying himself or herself with purchases. Whether it's a quick pop into Saks for a new handbag or a cheap pair of earrings at a craft fair (women disproportionately suffer from this problem), this spender buys for reasons that are more complex. If you fall into this latter category of Pathological Purchasers, you may simply need to be more self-aware or you may require serious help to quit a true addiction.

Before we move on, I want to clear up a common misconception. Many people who have completed this exercise told me they originally thought reducing their number of weekly purchases would simply force them to spend more per purchase. It wasn't immediately clear that the Weekly Purchase Total would cut out unnecessary expenditures–these skeptics simply assumed they would learn to buy more during their less-frequent trips to the store. But it won't take you long to realize that the majority of purchases you're eliminating are those that were completely unnecessary in the first place. Trust me (even you skeptics), you won't need to build more thorough shopping lists; you'll simply cut out superfluous spending.

You may find you can never do better than "Moderately Money-Minded," but that's okay–at the very least, you'll no longer be a victim of numb spending.

Note: If you live in an urban area where you do all your shopping on foot, or if you're someone who simply likes to buy the freshest produce each day, you're probably finding that you easily, and perhaps unfairly, fall into the "Pathological Purchaser" category.

I created the Weekly Purchases Scale with the suburban shopper in mind, but I'm also aware that as more people try to buy fresh and local, they may be less inclined to do all their grocery shopping in one weekly trip to the supermarket. Shopping for fresh produce or groceries on a daily basis is obviously different from random shopping every day. As a general rule of thumb, if your lifestyle requires you to shop daily for your grocery necessities, automatically subtract five to seven purchases from your total number of purchases. But be honest with yourself. Only subtract the number of daily grocery trips you make in order to bring your number in line with grocery shopping as a one-time purchase for the week. After all, the point of counting your purchases is to separate regular, necessary purchases from spontaneous ones.

CHAPTER
SIX

BUDGETING AND RELATIONSHIPS
(A GUIDE TO NOT SLEEPING ON THE COUCH)

YOUR FINANCIAL SUCCESS ISN'T SOLELY DEPENDENT ON YOUR OWN PERSONAL MASTERY.

Just when you think you've mastered your financial world and all will be well, you realize that your financial success isn't solely dependent on your own personal mastery. If you are married (or in a committed relationship), then your financial future is often linked to your ability to get along with your significant other. This isn't a choice. If you truly want to flourish, then you and your partner need to be on the same page to some degree.

Ever wanted an ex-spouse? Wait, don't answer that. I mean, do you want to help prevent future marital chaos? (There we go, much better.) Well, do you? You need to understand that money disagreements are rarely about money. Money arguments are usually about feelings and trust. And what's somewhat alarming is the fact if you don't trust your spouse with money, then you don't trust your spouse.

Don't freak out, though, and reach for your iPod to fire up Boys II Men's "End of the Road" (in my view, the perfect song for a breakup or death). There's still hope for your relationship. In fact, if you can recover from your financial trust issues, your relationship will be even stronger for it. Trust is earned through effort and opportunity. If you make financial trust a focus of your relationship, you can really strengthen your relationship as a whole. But that involves giving your partner an opportunity to earn your trust in return.

THE DEBATE OVER SEPARATE CHECKING ACCOUNTS

There is a very strange debate going on in America today that you may or may not be privy to. The debate is this: should married people have separate accounts to make life easier in the event of divorce?

It is a sad yet interesting argument. Should you live your financial life cautiously to protect yourself from getting wiped out in a divorce scenario? I have seen a number of instances when one spouse is left high and dry after a divorce. Could he or she have prevented this catastrophe by asking for separate accounts early in the marriage? Maybe, but is such caution a self-fulfilling prophecy? I honestly don't know the answer, but I do have an opinion. This is a very complicated predicament.

Married people with separate accounts are not a beacon of mistrust. In many instances separate accounts are a stress management technique. Oddly enough, I tripped into this epiphany. Mrs. Planner and I have had separate checking accounts for the last three years. We didn't intend for this to happen, but when we set out to switch banks a few years ago, we never fully completed the transfer. Thus, we kept two different checking accounts. We certainly don't have financial trust issues, so why do we bother keeping our money separate? It just works. The money is separated, however, the owners of the money remain the same. We both own the money. We both have "rights" to the money. Her paycheck dumps into "her" account for our use, and my paycheck dumps into "my" account for our use.

I use "my" account for the mortgage, charity, daycare, groceries, dining, and my fuel. She uses "her" account for the utilities, Target trips, car insurance, life insurance, her fuel, investing, and some other miscellaneous items. The reality is both accounts are for our benefit. I view my income as "our" income, and she views her income as "our" income. This is enough. There is no need to have one checking account to accomplish this financial nirvana. In the past, I incorrectly asserted that a joint checking account was a must to build marital trust. The reality is, though, it's often easier to split your money into two, and then split the bills into two. This is what Mrs. Planner and I have done and we have never had the slightest disagreement about who pays for what.

I'm not asking you to now split off into separate accounts. I'm asking you to find a system that works best for you. I do know what won't work: my money and your money. Separate accounts start to suck when the money in the account isn't the household's money, but instead it's for the sole usage of the account holder. In fact, that operating system will always end in disaster. The household's money doesn't always have to remain in a joint account, but always needs to be the household's money.

We all have different talents and skill sets. Some people are excellent spellers, while others can calculate a server's tip in their head in two seconds. Why am I pointing out the obvious? Realizing you and your significant other may have different money skills is one key to budgeting success.

Money stress within a marriage can turn your hair gray quickly. No two married people deal with money the same way. Rarely do both people physically pay bills, manage investments, and manage the household budget. And you know what? That's okay!

If you happen to be in a relationship that keeps separate finances, then that's okay…as long as your system truly works. You need to take an honest look at both partners and ensure that your separate account system is A) working and B) not a product of mistrust. If you feel good about the answers to those questions, then feel free to continue on your way.

GETTING MARRIED LATER IN LIFE

Americans are getting married at a later age these days. According to the CDC, "in 2006–2010, women and men married for the first time at older ages than in previous years. The median age at first marriage was 25.8 for women and 28.3 for men." Therefore, an individual's money habits have more time to develop. So when two 28-year-olds come together to get married, they instantly have a potential problem on their hands. Often, at least one of them is dealing with consumer debt and/or mediocre credit. And unfortunately, a person with excellent credit marrying someone with terrible credit does not equal average credit. It equals a major problem unless it's properly and promptly addressed. Old habits die hard, but they die harder when a new party is involved.

My wife and I were married right out of college, so we luckily entered the relationship with few financial problems. While we didn't have any debt, we did have different spending habits and methods of accounting for our spending. My wife always has been more frugal and disciplined than I am, whereas I've been looser with my money and accounting methods. Clearly, my own habits have changed—and yours can, too.

No matter your age when you get married, you should realize your financial habits are generally a product of your upbringing. This fact can have a long-lasting impact on your relationship. If your partner's parents struggled financially, then your partner will have a propensity to struggle financially. If your partner's parents lived an opulent lifestyle, then your partner is likely to want or expect a similar lifestyle.

If you address this potential issue properly and keep the lines of communication open, you can avoid the problems that may arise from this predicament.

LEARNING TO MAKE DECISIONS AS A COUPLE

You want to save for a family vacation next summer. Your significant other wants to pay off the credit card bill from the previous vacation. Who is right? Who is less right? And how do you come to a decision together without someone sleeping in the guest bedroom? (Not that I've ever slept in the guest bedroom. The light is so pretty coming through the curtains in the morning in that room. I always enjoy it.)

Most people think their ideas are right. Otherwise, you wouldn't think what you are thinking. You generally don't set out thinking about something knowing you are wrong. And even when you do, you justify your wrong thoughts so they appear outwardly right. Example? If you have ever said, "I work hard, so I deserve it," then you most likely are trying to cover up a bad idea with weak justification. If there wasn't a question on whether or not you could afford something, then you wouldn't have to break out the "I deserve it" argument. This idea is hard enough to deal with as an individual. Now, add your significant other into the equation, and you have two people, two brains, two sets of thoughts, two ideas of affordability, and two sets of justifications that affect affordability.

The only way to address this confusion waiting to happen is to have joint financial goals. Without goals, you are wandering around aimlessly in a financial world that is poised to kick your arse. Please understand that the operative word in the phrase "joint financial goals" is joint. Individual financial goals are great and all, but they aren't really going to help your relationship that much. You need joint financial goals. Do not ignore this advice. If you have ever said, "We aren't on the same page financially," then joint financial goals will at least put you in the same book. Beyond that, holding each other accountable to your joint goals will put you in the same chapter.

So, the advice: sit down with your significant other and create financial goals you both agree on. Believe it or not, this is also where you need to practice the art of compromise. It's likely that one person is more financially focused. If this is the case, then allow the not-as-focused person to speak his or her mind. I believe it was Sir Elton John who once said, "Don't dampen the flame of a flickering candle in the wind." Okay, I made that up. But my point is the person "struggling" needs to do most of the sharing, not the person who "knows what he/she is talking about." Constant hammering away by the person in-the-know is counterproductive. You'd be surprised how much progress you can make when the "not great with money" person gets to talk.

P.E.T.E CAN HELP

The most effective way to develop the money relationship with your significant other is to employ "P.E.T.E." (Yes, I'm that vain.): Patience, Equality, Trust, and Effort.

PATIENCE. Relationships require patience. Understanding money concepts comes more easily to some people than to others. Be patient with those who need a little more help than you do. Your patience will be rewarded with meaningful cooperation.

EQUALITY. As my dad's best friend used to say, "Don't be a jerk." Being n a committed relationship with shared finances in the twenty-first century means both partners are equal. Men and women share almost every responsibility in today's home. So unless you're sporting a loincloth and a mangy beard, be prepared to share in the work. It doesn't matter who makes more money. It doesn't matter who went farther in school. You are equal.

TRUST. Relationships are nothing without trust. You don't trust your partner if you don't trust him or her with money. The solution to a lack of trust when it comes to money is good communication. Work together, and the trust will follow. A variation on the Golden Rule works best: trust as you wish to be trusted. In fact, while you're at it, treat money the way you want it to treat you.

EFFORT. Think how long it takes to plan a week's vacation. Most people put more effort into that one week than they do in planning their financial future. Financial prosperity is not meant for lazy people. Trying is the first step, but doing is the goal. As the Jedi Master Yoda once said, "Do, or do not. There is no try." Developing your relationship when it comes to money is not easy. That's why some people are reluctant to try.

THE SAVELATERS AND THE CAREYS

These case studies, based on real-life people, will help you identify poor but common money habits. The names of these clients have been changed to protect the guilty.

AL AND ALMA SAVELATER

Take a look at Al and Alma Savelater's money situation, and see if you can identify any obvious mistakes.

Al and Alma Savelater quick facts:
- They both are 32 years old.
- Al is addicted to golf.
- Alma is a frugal bargain hunter.
- They have two children, aged six and eight.
- Their combined household income is $80,000 (Al makes $55,000; Alma takes home $25,000).

Al and Alma have three separate checking accounts. Al's paycheck is directly deposited into one account; Alma's paycheck in directly deposited into another account, and they each make equal contributions to a third account, which is used to pay the major monthly bills.

The remainder of the Savelaters' money is left in their own personal accounts to be used at their individual discretion. Because Al makes more money, he decides to give $100 per month to Alma as an "allowance." (I call this a reparations payment.) A different person pays every time they go out to eat. They argue about how much to spend on a gift for a relative, and they bicker about who is going to pay for it. Their children sense that something is amiss, but they can't put their sticky little fingers on it. Al and Alma each make contributions to the children's college funds, but they do it separately.

There are some important facts missing in Al and Alma's case. Alma doesn't trust Al implicitly. Al entered the marriage with quite a bit of debt, and later they had to refinance their house to pay it off. Meanwhile, Al believes he can make most of the money decisions by himself because he makes most of the money. Al shuts down when Alma brings up money. He completely loses his patience when his wife questions his spending. He often takes out large ATM cash withdrawals so he doesn't have to be held accountable for his cash spending.

Do you see the potential problems here? Does it seem as though they are setting up their finances to one day separate their relationship?

KERRY AND CARRIE CAREY

Meet Kerry and Carrie Carey. This redundant couple has a tendency to make the same mistakes over and over again.

Kerry and Carrie Carey quick facts:
- Kerry works for a copy company and just got his MBA.
- Carrie works as a nurse in a fertility clinic.
- They both work in the reproduction field.
- They just got married.
- They both just graduated from grad school.
- They have a combined $60,000 worth of student loans.
- They just bought a condo.
- They just bought a new car with a 48-month loan.
- They just bought $2,500 worth of furniture at twelve months same-as-cash financing.

Kerry and Carrie couldn't be more excited about having two steady paychecks. They are delighted to be married and are eager to begin a new life together. They worked their way through college and have just $60,000 in student loans, even though their combined educations cost a total of $132,000.

Kerry and Carrie never talk about money. The topic stresses them out, so they avoid it. Who wants to talk about something that creates so much discomfort? They believe all of their problems will be solved once they start making more money. Besides, they have graduate degrees, so pay increases are right around the corner, right?

Kerry and Carrie are representative of many graduate-school professionals. They have bright futures–but are living on their presumed future income instead of their present income.

Living on an income that currently does not exist is a huge problem for ambitious people fresh out of college and graduate school. There is a school of thought that claims you should "fake it till you make it"–but this method never accounts for developing ever-important savings habits.

The Savelaters and the Careys could have used the power of P.E.T.E.

Remember, no one cares more about your success than you do. You need to be the person who asks for change. P.E.T.E. can't force you to care, but P.E.T.E. will help you become a better spouse, and hopefully P.E.T.E. will keep you from sleeping on the couch.

Here are a few final tips to keep your relationship headed in the right direction.

DON'T EVER HAVE A SPONTANEOUS MONEY CONVERSATION

They are pointless. It is impossible for a spontaneous conversation about money to turn out positively. In most cases, the other person is rarely prepared to have the conversation, and may react like a badger stuck in a shoebox. Instead, ask to have a planned money discussion, a few days in advance. That way, everyone can "get their mind right" (as my football coach used to say). Use the Ideal Household Budget to help steer the conversation.

OFFER AN OLIVE BRANCH

Nobody is financially perfect. And even if you are the person who is "good with money" (a ridiculous premise, by the way), some financial habit of yours probably annoys your partner, too. During your planned money conversation, address your annoying habit, and demonstrate your willingness to work on it.

This process will lead to tough conversations, but trust me, tough conversations are better than avoiding the topic altogether. When both of you take responsibility for your finances, you begin to make progress. The good news is that your monthly meetings ultimately will get a lot easier.

CHAPTER
SEVEN
A MONTHLY
BUDGETING
MEETING
WILL MAKE THE
DIFFERENCE

A LOT OF ENERGY GOES INTO BUDGETING.

Over the last few chapters, you've learned many of the nuances of creating and maintaining a monthly budget. With surprise expenses, surpluses, shortages, price targets, and the creation of the budget itself, a lot of energy goes into budgeting. That should speak volumes about its level of importance in your financial life. The monthly budget meeting should reinforce this idea.

A monthly budget meeting is a time to sit down with your significant other (or other person who is directly affected by your spending habits), evaluate your financial decisions from the previous month, and project upcoming budgetary adjustments/considerations.

The goal in budgeting always is to increase your awareness, communication, and accountability. Nowhere are these three concepts more apparent than in your monthly budget meeting. Let's take just a moment to look at how each concept comes into play.

AWARENESS:

You're no doubt familiar with my feelings about the positive effects of awareness on your financial decisions. When you place awareness alongside a discussion with someone else about your finances during your monthly budget meetings, you create something I like to call hyper-awareness. It's similar to what happens when you take a project you've been working on in private out to the general public. It helps you begin to evaluate your project critically through others' eyes. When it comes to the budget meeting, hyper-awareness is good because it forces you to view your actions from a completely different perspective than you would have otherwise.

COMMUNICATION:

A constructive financial discussion often involves either admitting your own struggles or being on the receiving end of somebody else's admission (or denial) of the same. It's odd to think that people who know each other intimately have trouble talking about money, but because our culture places so much weight on financial stability, it can be a very sensitive topic. I've seen many cases where, in order to avoid addressing a loved one's issues, one partner in a relationship will volunteer himself or herself to take control of and try to compensate for the other's finances. This tactic, however, can have very severe and lasting effects on a relationship. Taking responsibility for somebody else's actions can transform existing roles in the relationship, thereby changing the dynamic of the relationship as a whole. What might seem like a kind and loving gesture can ultimately be the cause of real resentment for all involved.

From the moment you begin sharing financial responsibility with another person, you must open the lines of communication and work together to solve any existing issues. A planned budget meeting between you and your partner is an ideal way of preventing a spontaneous money conversation. (In other words, a fight.)

ACCOUNTABILITY:

Examining your spending every month with the person who also is affected by your decisions is a surefire way to increase your level of accountability for your actions. If you're in a partnership, both people will be under the same amount of pressure, which is good, because as I noted earlier, it's not enough for one half of a couple to be accountable while the other half passively stands by. You'll quickly figure out which decisions advance your goals and which ones are only hindering your ultimate financial aspirations.

In summary, awareness, communication, and accountability are all key components of what should become a regular ritual for anyone who shares financial responsibilities with someone else.

This brings us to the point of this chapter: planning your first monthly budget meeting.

THE MEETING

Your monthly budget meeting will have three participants: you, your significant other, and your budget. It should take place within the first five days of the month, and the topic should be your spending in the previous month. In order to assess your spending, you'll need your detailed checking account statements and credit card statements (both of which you can print out using your bank's online banking system), and any other spending activity statements from that month.

One person will be responsible for reading aloud each transaction, line by line, while the other person will be responsible for recording each item in the appropriate category of your budget. You can download a free budget template by visiting *PeteThePlanner. com/BudgetTemplate*

As you read through these statements together, each of you will no doubt need to justify a number of your purchases and scrutinize those that don't contribute to your financial goals. You may cringe at the thought of openly airing your personal finances with your partner, but you need to bite the bullet. Only by honestly discussing your spending habits alongside your financial goals can you make honest assessments and begin to eliminate unnecessary or excessive spending.

THINGS TO LOOK FOR:

- Overspending
- Bills you forgot to pay
- Loans/debts you finished paying in the previous month
- Places where you might be able to reduce your monthly spending beyond the 10% you trimmed when you established price targets
- Budget projections that were far off-track (whether positively or negatively)
- Strange spending patterns. For instance, do you go to the same place every Wednesday without realizing it?
- Discrepancies you can dispute with your bank
- Proper credit for merchandise you returned

THINGS TO ADJUST:

- Price targets
- New expenses you need to add
- Items that have been paid off and thus need to be removed
- Savings deposits that are affected by money you've freed up after paying off a loan or other debt
- Surprise bills you didn't add previously

Your budget is not static. It will likely change at least a little bit each month, ideally to account for improvements.

The best part of these monthly meetings is that practice makes perfect. The more meetings you have, the faster they go. You actually will begin to look forward to finding out whether you had a good month or a bad month. Your meeting should last less than thirty minutes; by the end of that time, you will be able to identify your surplus or shortage.

SURPLUS VS. SHORTAGE

One of the main reasons for maintaining a monthly budget is to determine whether the previous month produced a shortage or a surplus. Just as every business should know whether the previous month produced positive or negative earnings, individuals should be aware of their own monthly peaks and valleys. Not knowing where you stand each month could lead to serious financial hardship. It's time to start thinking of your household–or at least the financial parts of it–as a business.

Remember, there's nothing wrong with having neither a surplus nor a shortage if you've met all of your financial obligations for the month. This simply means you have done a good job budgeting. "Yes, Pete," you're saying. "I know what surpluses and shortages are. Can I skip this part?" No. We're going to go beyond simply knowing what these terms mean; we're going to explore how to think about them and how to apply them to your overall financial strategy. The good news is we're going to get through all of that rather quickly.

SURPLUSES

Surpluses result from not spending all the money you've made in a given month, during that month. A surplus is the amount of money left over after paying all of your bills and allocating money to the investment and savings categories you've identified in your budget: emergency fund(s), a savings account, life insurance, and/or other investments. Assuming you've met these monthly obligations, a surplus opens opportunities for you. It's a powerful tool that can and should be used to accomplish your long-term financial goals.

So what should you do with your surpluses?

1. Pay off debt. This means going above and beyond the monthly payment of any outstanding balances.
2. Save the money for an upcoming "expensive" month. Many times, surpluses are fleeting rather than regular. If this month's surplus is a one-off—maybe due to a bonus or monetary gift— the best thing to do is to set the extra cash aside for a less-fortunate month or even for a surprise bill you didn't account for, despite your better efforts.
3. Put the money into long-term savings. If you've paid off your debt and you can safely say this surplus will be consistent and representative of your financial situation for months, or even years, to come, it's time to get serious about your long-term savings. You may want to set up monthly automatic savings, for example. And if this is something you're already taking advantage of, consider increasing your monthly deposits to that savings account.

If you consistently have a surplus, yes, you can be slightly more lenient with your spending.

MAKING SAVINGS A BILL

Which of these do you like best: the electric company, the credit card company, the hospital, or yourself? It's not a trick question, so go ahead and answer. That's right. It's you.

Well, if you love yourself so much more than you love those other guys, then why do you send them money every month but you don't send yourself any? I'm not talking about your 401(k) or any other pre-tax investment. I'm talking about having money automatically transferred from your checking account into an investment or savings account.

The most important part of saving money is developing the habit. If you can only save $50 per month at the outset, do it. Don't wait to begin until you have a lot of money to save, because you'll never do it.

You need to teach yourself the habit of saving. You don't learn to ride a motorcycle before you learn to ride a bicycle. No, you first have to develop the necessary skills before strapping on a helmet and jumping on that crotch rocket.

This particular step of the budgeting process is not optional. But it is the most-ignored means of building wealth.

Making your monthly savings a bill, in effect, accomplishes two key objectives. First, it helps you accumulate money. Second, it teaches you to live on less. By accomplishing these two objectives, you succeed on both sides. You are trimming expenses and building cash reserves at the same time. Bottom line: this is the most fiscally responsible activity you can engage in.

WHY MOST BUDGETING SOFTWARE AND WEBSITES WILL FAIL YOU

My smart phone can schedule my week, let me surf the Internet, play music, record music, display videos, play games, wake me up in the morning, take pictures, take video, and sync with the computer in my car–but all these features don't necessarily make my life easier.

Like most people, I am distracted by all the bells and whistles; I see shiny sparkly things, and I lose my mind. Despite their popularity, I find that most budgeting websites cause the same problem: they provide convenience, but they don't provide enough behavior-changing opportunities.

Most financial software/websites (their names are being withheld to protect...me) are way too complicated and give you much more information than you need. The truth of your current financial situation often is misrepresented and the software/website takes almost weekly, if not daily, maintenance on your part.

But the strangest disadvantage of using a packaged software system or website is it ignores two of the three vital purposes of my budgeting system.

They are:
1. To bring financial awareness to every situation.
2. To improve spousal communication with regard to money.
3. To promote accountability in your household.

The software and websites only bring financial awareness. They do nothing to improve communication with your partner or promote accountability. The awareness they do bring often can be over-whelming. What ultimately makes a good money month a good money month? The answer: bringing in more than you spend. It's that simple. Yes, some other details and data are nice, but the reality is most people who aren't saving money ignore the simplest of concepts. They are too distracted by self-populating budgeting charts that take communication out of the equation.

Let's say your spouse went to the same restaurant twelve times in one month. If you are using one of the many popular budgeting websites, then the aggregate spending total will just show up in the dining expense category. Your spouse's egregious error goes completely undetected. They know they have a problem, but you don't. A thorough budget meeting will sniff this out, and rectify the problem. How do I know this? Because Mrs. Planner once discovered that I ate lunch out at the same restaurant 19 times in one month. Busted.

So relax, light some candles, and start budgeting.
Wine, candles, soft music, and ... budgeting?

READY... SET... TALK

Now that your categories are set up and you and your spouse are alone together in a room with your materials in hand, it's time to begin. One person should man the computer, while the other person should be armed with the statements and highlighters.

First, go through and highlight your major recurring categories with a different highlighter color. These major categories are usually groceries, dining, and fuel. These are the categories you will enter first into your budget template. You then go through your statements and systematically key in the data for each transaction.

The first time my wife and I held a budget meeting, we were shocked. We couldn't believe how many times we spent money over the course of a month. We averaged three to four debit-card transactions per day. We had a general idea of how much money we spent, but we didn't know the frequency of our expenditures. While we were good about making savings a bill, we didn't do a good job of saving a surplus. But once we began talking about our budget every month, we were able to significantly improve our already good financial situation.

After you have entered all of your expenditures and deposits into the template, you will have two main large numbers. The net of these numbers is your surplus or your shortage.

Next, talk with your spouse. What is coming up next month? What potentially large expenditures are on the horizon? How many times are you getting paid next month?

I don't want to alarm you or anything, but you just talked about money...with your spouse. Whether you had a shortage or a surplus, you are now better off. You have opened the lines of communication. You have learned more about your current financial situation. You have taken personal responsibility for your financial standing.

SETTING PRICE TARGETS

By now you've made it through some of the most challenging aspects of budgeting–namely, comparing your spending to The Ideal Budget and tackling bad habits that can cripple your budget. The next step? Setting the parameters that will help you regulate your spending in all areas of your life.

One useful set of parameters is price targets, the spending limits you assign to each item in your budget. Essentially, establishing price targets is a fancy way of describing the act of setting individual budgets for each item on your budget, based on your monthly obligations and income. Think of price targets as "mini-budgets."

Your goal is to keep your monthly spending less than or equal to the target amounts you set for each item, in order to keep your overall monthly budget on track. Done correctly, price targets allow you to create several small victories every month.

GENERATING PRICE TARGETS

1) Start by calculating the three-month spending average for each item in your budget. (Don't try to set price targets using just one month's data. You'll end up with skewed numbers.) Some items in your budget are fixed, such as your car payment and your rent or mortgage. Go ahead and enter the price targets anyway. When you pay off a car or some other expense, you will easily be able to take the money you've budgeted for said item and save it.

2) Take the average for each item and reduce it by 10% to identify your price targets. Why 10%? Well, people tend to waste money. So much money, in fact, that the vast majority of us can reduce our spending by 10% without feeling a thing. By cutting 10%, you simply trim the fat off your price targets, rather than cut into your needs. Think of it as streamlining your spending. Don't freak out if this number doesn't seem like a realistic amount. It will take some time to get your spending down to the price target, but you need to remain consistently focused.

For instance, let's say you have determined that your average monthly grocery costs over the last three months were $400. Here is what your calculation might look like:

JANUARY ($500) + FEBRUARY ($400) + MARCH ($300) = $1,200.

$1,200 DIVIDED BY 3 MONTHS = $400 PER MONTH.

SUBTRACT 10% ($40): $400 PER MONTH MINUS 10% ($40) = $360.

This means your price target for groceries is $360. Your goal now is to keep your spending for your grocery category under the target of $360. (For concrete strategies on how to become a smarter, more efficient shopper in order to stay within your price target, revisit Chapter 3.) Price targets help you reduce spending because they break your spending into manageable, attainable increments. While you might have trouble keeping track of how your grocery bills fit into your overall budget, you'll find it's much easier to see how they fit into your monthly grocery price target.

Once you've taken the time to establish each of your category price targets, you will want to address them during your monthly budget meetings with your significant other. Once a month, you will compare your actual spending to the price target as a means of tracking your discipline and your progress toward your financial goals. If you spend less than your price target, you'll improve your chances for an overall monthly budget surplus.

Try applying this to your own budget. Let's look at your average monthly entertainment spending, for example. Plug your costs into the formula to determine your price target.

MONTH 1 ($) + MONTH 2 ($) + MONTH 3 ($) = $.

$ (THE TOTAL FROM THE FIRST LINE)
DIVIDED BY 3 MONTHS = $ PER MONTH.

SUBTRACT 10% FROM THE TOTAL FROM THE SECOND LINE ($):

TAKE THE TOTAL FROM THE SECOND LINE AND
SUBTRACT THE TOTAL FROM THE LINE ABOVE: $.

YOUR PRICE TARGET FOR ENTERTAINMENT IS $
(THE TOTAL FROM THE LINE ABOVE).

It's crucial to constantly strive to do better with your price targets. If you come in under your price target for three months in a row, then lower the target another 10%. The more often you come in under the price target, the more quickly you'll accomplish your financial goals.

A monthly budget meeting is the best way to stay on top of your finances. You will open the lines of communication, become more aware of your financial standing, and hold each other accountable to your goals. There are no shortcuts to success. There are no computer programs that will solve your problems. Keep in mind: your goal during these meetings is to effectively manage your income to create a surplus. You owe it to yourselves.

ONE LAST IMPORTANT POINT

Do it today.

CHAPTER
EIGHT
BUDGET
FOR
GOOD

BUDGETING IS A SKILL YOU WILL USE YOUR ENTIRE ADULT LIFE.

Your decision to budget will not go unnoticed. Budgeting is a skill you will use your entire adult life. In fact, budgeting is not only the key to affording your working life, but it's also the key to affording your retirement lifestyle. You must become proficient at budgeting now. Waiting to learn to budget in the years preceding retirement is incredibly difficult. Teaching an old dog new tricks is actually quite challenging.

While I can't shape your financial motivation, I would like to offer you some financial thoughts contrary to conventional financial wisdom. The budgeting tips in this book will allow you to afford more. When you can control spending in problem categories, then you can spend that previously wasted money on new and different things. But should you? Should you use your newfound budgeting acumen to fund a consumption-based lifestyle? In my opinion, no. I don't believe you should be in a constant struggle to afford more. I believe true success comes in needing less. Need is such a subjective concept. There is something beautiful about a very simple financial life.

If abstract philosophizing doesn't work for you, then maybe some mind-boggling numbers will. Let's for a moment assume you start your work life at age 20 and end your work life at age 60. Let's also assume you live to age 100. This means your 40 years of work need to fund 80 years of living. The money you earn via work from ages 20-60 must not only fund your lifestyle from ages 20-60, but you also must earn and save enough to fund your retirement from ages 60-100. How can you possibly achieve this when material accumulation is your aim? I don't think you can. As our longevity increases, so will the need for budgeting. When retirement lasted 5-10 years, budgeting was hardly an issue. Today, the irony is that your insistence on wanting to afford more may result in not being able to afford to live a long life.

YOU MUST REPRIORITIZE

What are your financial priorities? You only have so much money. You only have so much time. And you only have so much brain space. Unfortunately, I've found many people don't realize this. One of the most discrete, yet ominous mistakes people make on a regular basis: the failure to deprioritize appropriately.

For example, I often come across couples who claim their number one priority is education for their children. In fact, they generally utter the exact words, "Education for our children is our number one priority." The problem starts, however, in that their previous financial priority before children was a car, the perfect house, or an expensive craft beer habit. When you are committed to a previous fancy car lifestyle, tied to an expensive mortgage, or are unwilling to put your fermented beverage fetish behind you, then your new "spoken" priority isn't really a priority at all. This doesn't make you silly, stupid, or dishonorable. It makes you human. If you've spent ten years making one thing your priority, it's incredibly difficult to make a change to a new one.

There are many steps you can take to prevent this scenario from happening, but unfortunately there isn't a ton you can do if it has already happened to you. Let's say you have committed a great deal of your two-income household income to your perfect home mortgage payment. And now let's say you decide you want to be a stay-at-home dad and raise your children in this perfect home. The problem is obvious. It will be damn near impossible to stay at home with your children when your income is so vital in being able to afford your home. The solution isn't to ignore the problem and hope it goes away. The solution is so overwhelming that most people aren't willing to do it. The solution is to sell your home, and raise your children in a lesser home. The solution isn't to "make it work." I know this is a hypothetical example, but unfortunately making it work rarely really works.

Here's a very simple exercise. Speak your number one financial priority aloud right now. It's okay. What words slipped through your lips when you asked your brain to produce your financial priority? Excellent. Next question. Do you act like it? Do you treat your number one priority as your number one priority, or are you still treating your five-years-ago-number-one-priority as your number one priority?

What's even more surprising is when you realize that, in practice, your number one priority isn't something you intended. Did you trade in an upside down (negative equity) car? This would mean you financed your new car for more than it was worth because you had to finance in what you still owed on your old car. The result of all this rigmarole is your transportation budget requires a disproportionate amount of your household income. Therefore, you may be treating your car as your number one financial priority and not even realize it.

And what's even crazier is when you justify a borrowing decision by claiming it's your number one financial priority, yet then do everything in your power to ignore the debt that comes with this priority. You guessed it. I'm talking about student loans.

Where do you stand? Is your number one spoken priority your number one priority in practice?

THERE'S A DIFFERENCE BETWEEN BEING PATIENT AND WAITING

As strange as it sounds, I've seen several people ruin their financial lives by simply waiting. Yet, I've also seen several people become financially successful by simply being patient. There are major differences in waiting and being patient. Here are examples of both.

WAITING

- "I'll start saving next year, once I'm making more money."
- "I'll put a budget together if things get tight."
- "I'll pay off my student loans later."
- "I'll pay back my parents when they put heat on me."
- "I'll set money aside for taxes later in the year."
- "I'll get life insurance when I get older."
- "I'll be charitable when I become wealthy."

PATIENCE

- "I'll buy the house I can afford now, not the house I want."
- "I'll trade-in my car once it's paid off, not while I still owe money on it."
- "I'll take the proper amount of investment risk now, and not be too risky for no good reason."
- "I'll buy clothes I can afford without a store credit card."
- "I'll go on vacation when I can pre-fund it."

It's all about attitude. Waiting for arbitrary events never gets you anywhere. If you are constantly waiting for time to pass, then you will miss out on opportunity. Take control of your financial future by eliminating arbitrary time measures. Don't wait. Be patient.

BE SURE THAT YOU ARE RELYING ON THE RIGHT SATISFIER

I'm convinced that self-induced financial problems are the result of misunderstanding one's self. I think people who put themselves in severe financial distress are looking for satisfaction in things money can't buy, yet they use money, often money they don't have, in an effort to buy happiness.

Let's first examine satisfaction. Satisfaction occurs when you are fulfilled or gratified. We can feel this sensation in a number of ways. We can be satisfied when we finish a tedious project. We can be satisfied when we receive compliments. We can be satisfied when we achieve an athletic goal. Yet, the most common vehicle of satisfaction is commerce. And this usually occurs when we are unsatisfied and are trying to get satisfied. Next, let's examine what caused your dissatisfaction. Was it your job? Was it your marriage? Was it your financial situation? To me, this is the most important part of the satisfaction problem. If you are constantly spending money in order to feel fulfilled, then what is it making you feel so damn empty in the first place? If you can identify this issue, then you should be able to curb your spending. Yes, this is a higher level conversation. Believe it or not, no matter how much you want that $1000 purse or that $5000 TV, there is something else that would satisfy you much more than either of these things. And this thing will cost you absolutely nothing.

Here's the test. For a moment, assume everything you want is free. Your house is free. Your food is free. And all of your clothes are free. Do you feel fulfilled? Absolutely not. It may bring temporary happiness, but it is far from fulfilling. The cause of your dissatisfaction is not addressed when you separate items from their price tags. Thus, the cause of your dissatisfaction cannot be absolved via supplementation. You can't add things to your life to remove dissatisfaction. You can try to do this, but you still will always be dissatisfied at your core.

I've seen several people stay in jobs they hated simply because they were paid tremendous amounts of money. They used this money to try to relieve their dissatisfaction. The more they bought, the more frustrated they got at how dissatisfied they were. Sometimes this became obvious in just a couple of years, but it most often took 10-20 years to figure it out. The temptation in reading this idea is to think, "But if they quit their job, then they can't afford the house and the lifestyle they currently have." You are correct if you are thinking this. However, my argument is people who are truly satisfied won't care if they can't have the things that formerly temporarily satisfied them.

If you are thinking, "I couldn't possibly be satisfied with less house or less money," then just know you are in the majority. But think about it for a moment; the fulfillment in your life doesn't have to come from things. If you don't think you will be satisfied with fewer things, you are wrong. In my opinion, you have created a life in which things have become your measure of satisfaction. This isn't a permanent problem, though. And the crazy thing is it's not that hard to correct. It takes a while to get there mentally, but the adjustment itself is simple.

I speak from experience. In 2007 I made more money than I had ever earned before, or have ever earned since. But, I was very dissatisfied. I achieved fulfillment by spending the money I made on superfluous items. Some five years later I make much less money, and I don't really care. I don't measure my success by my tax return. I'm very satisfied, and money really has nothing to do with it. In fact, I believe my satisfaction actually enhances my ability to make money. Whereas my income will eventually reach 2007 levels sometime in the near future, I don't really care. I'll continue to give money to the causes I care about, and continue to take away money's power over me. Enough about me. This isn't about me, this is about you.

Look at your current financial stress point. Is it the result of seeking satisfaction in the wrong things? Were you trying to seek satisfaction in order to replace an ever-present feeling of dissatisfaction? If this process has put you in the hole, then you have some scrapping to do in order to get back to even. Once you solve your financial problems, then you can start to make big choices on satisfaction and dissatisfaction.

This isn't necessarily about changing jobs, but it could be. It also could be about getting healthy, repairing relationships, or renewing your spiritual health. Sometimes the best way to be satisfied is to remove what is so dissatisfying.

WHERE DO FINANCIAL PROBLEMS AND CHARACTER INTERSECT?

Character n.
1. the aggregate of features and traits that form the individual nature of some person or thing.
2. one such feature or trait; characteristic.
3. moral or ethical quality: a man of fine, honorable character.
4. qualities of honesty, courage, or the like; integrity: It takes character to face up to a bully.
5. reputation: a stain on one's character.

Are financial problems the result of a poor character? Sometimes they are, but not always. Are financial problems the result of character flaws? Not all the time, but many times. We all have character flaws. We just hate being called out for them.

We shouldn't try to avoid discussing our character flaws, and we also shouldn't deny their affect on our decision-making.

What sort of character flaws directly affect our financial lives? Well, there are many. Unrealistic optimism is an often ignored flaw. Conscious ignorance of warning signs has taken down many people. Materialism is quite an awful problem-causer. The inability to work together with a significant other will ruin any financial situation. A refusal to look toward the financial future has its challenges. An inability to show restraint and say "no" will get just about anyone in trouble. And the list goes on and on.

However, there are obvious situations in which significant financial problems are not caused by character flaws. If you had a sudden job loss or you came out on the wrong side of a medical problem or divorce, then it's obvious your character or character flaws aren't the primary cause of the problem. On the other hand, day-to-day financial problems such as credit card debt, a lack of savings, and an inability to afford your lifestyle, are, in fact, a result of character flaws. Something inside of you led to the decisions you have made. Don't ignore this fact. Don't ignore the presence of character flaws. Accept responsibility for your character, accept responsibility for your decision-making, and then accept responsibility for your financial situation.

The financial mistakes that are a result of character flaws aren't permanent mistakes, in most instances. In fact, these mistakes allow us to build character. These mistakes give us the opportunity to dig ourselves out of the holes our character flaws have dug. I can tell you with 100% certainty that over the last 14 years in the financial business, the greatest financial stories I have seen are stories of redemption and rebirth. Our mistakes don't have to define us, but our response to our mistakes will. My point is a simple one: look within your financial life and try to see if any of your financial problems are the result of character flaws. Then work on those flaws, and alleviate the problems these flaws caused. We must always be aware of our character flaws. They will cause problems, financial or otherwise, our entire lives. Acknowledge them, and work on them.

ONE FINAL NOTE

Use your knowledge of budgeting for good.
Budgeting will allow you to live on less, if
you so choose. I'm asking you to choose this.
Whether you are providing for yourself or
for your family, eliminating falsely perceived
needs will serve you well. I believe this is
*What Your Dad Never Taught You About
Budgeting.*

ABOUT THE AUTHOR

Peter Dunn (a.k.a. Pete the Planner), is responsible for some of the most cutting edge financial advice around. Whether he is preventing high income earners from wasting their opportunities or teaching single parents how to raise financially adjusted children, Pete the Planner always arrives to the scene with his trademark comedic wit.

He released the first edition of *What Your Dad Never Taught You About Budgeting* in 2006 and is the host of the popular radio show, The Pete the Planner Show, on 93 WIBC FM. He was also the mastermind behind 24 Hour News 8's 60 Days to Change and has appeared regularly on Fox News, Fox Business, CNN Headline News and numerous nationally syndicated radio programs. In January 2012, Cision named him the fourth most influential personal finance broadcaster in the United States.

His second book, *60 Days to Change: A Daily How To Guide With Actionable Tips to Improve Your Financial Life*, was released in December of 2009. His third book, *Avoid Student Loans*, was released in January 2012.

Peter was named one of "Indy's Best and Brightest" in finance in 2007 and in media in 2009 by KPMG and was declared one of NUVO Magazine's "30 under 30 to Watch in the Arts" for comedy (back when he was young and funny). Peter was awarded the Distinguished Alumni Award by Hanover College in 2012.

When not wrapped up in writing or dabbling in broadcast, Pete the Planner enjoys cooking and spending time with his wife Sarah and his children Ollie and Teddy.

You can learn more at *PeteThePlanner.com*

12174225R00100

Made in the USA
San Bernardino, CA
09 June 2014